My name is Lorraine Knight and I have been blessed with so many wonderful experiences. From a young child through to adulthood, I have been given so much proof of the spiritual beings around us. I believe that no-one should live in fear of the energies that accompany us through life.

Through the simplicity of love I have learnt that we are capable of so much more than we realise. Serving spiritual churches and centres in Kent, I try to bring this to others in a loving and gentle way.

God is in My Garden

Lorraine Knight

God is in My Garden

Olympia Publishers
London

www.olympiapublishers.com
OLYMPIA PAPERBACK EDITION

Copyright © Lorraine Knight 2014

The right of Lorraine Knight to be identified as author of this work has been asserted in accordance with sections 77 and 78 of the Copyright, Designs and Patents Act 1988.

All Rights Reserved

No reproduction, copy or transmission of this publication may be made without written permission.
No paragraph of this publication may be reproduced, copied or transmitted save with the written permission of the publisher, or in accordance with the provisions of the Copyright Act 1956 (as amended).

Any person who commits any unauthorised act in relation to this publication may be liable to criminal prosecution and civil claims for damage.

A CIP catalogue record for this title is available from the British Library.

ISBN: 978-1-84897-383-1

(Olympia Publishers is part of Ashwell Publishing Ltd)

First Published in 2014

Olympia Publishers
60 Cannon Street
London
EC4N 6NP

Printed in Great Britain

I dedicate this book to my sons Richard, Glen and Ben.
Never give up on your dreams.

Acknowledgements

I would like to thank my Mum for her continued support and encouragement in everything that I have put together. Also my good friends Christine and Steve, whose expertise has made this book happen.

Where there is love there is life

Contents

Prologue   19

Chapter One   21
My Garden

Chapter 2   25
David

Chapter 3   29
School

Chapter 4   33
Terrified

Chapter 5   36
Imagination

Chapter 6   39
A new beginning

Chapter 7   43
Mum

Chapter 8   47
Tree spirits

Chapter 9 50
Pop

Chapter 10 53
The worst film ever

Chapter 11 55
Denise

Chapter 12 58
Married life

Chapter 13 61
There must be more to life

Chapter 14 66
Healing

Chapter 15 70
Small steps

Chapter 16 76
A wonderful energy

Chapter 17 81
If I can do it, you can too

Chapter 18 88
My daughter

Chapter 19 92
Who am I?

Chapter 20   95
Protection

Chapter 21   100
Ben

Chapter 22   103
Trance and rescue

Chapter 23   109
Visitors at Night

Chapter 24   115
Love overcomes all

Chapter 25   123
Psychic Attack

Chapter 26   128
The Violet Flame

Chapter 27   136
Astral Rescues and healing

Chapter 28   139
Angels everywhere

Chapter 29   142
Unicorns

Prologue

There is so much more to life than we realise, so many wonderful things that are occurring all around us, and a lot of people are blind to this through fear or lack of understanding. I realise that now, and how I wish that I had remembered that as I grew up. It would have saved me so much trouble. Thousands upon thousands of beings drawn close to us, waiting to help us in every way possible. They come as children, animals, angels and many other creatures. Their purpose is to teach us that we have everything within us to make our lives complete. They help us reconnect with the important things around us, but most importantly they give us someone to talk to when we are sad and alone. As we learn to trust in our spirit friends, we must also learn to trust in ourselves. Through the love that they give us, we realise at some point that there is not one human beyond God's love, and not one person upon the Earth is more worthy than the other. To know that whatever we go through in our lives, there is always a reason for it. That reason is to help us grow spiritually and become an oasis of peace in a world that is sometimes very chaotic,

Fear is such a huge barrier and it takes a lot of courage to melt the fear away. But with constant love and support from the many spirits and people that come into our lives, we realise that the more we learn the less we fear. I've had to get over so much fear to deal with certain things in my life, things I never dreamt I would deal with. I'm not saying that they were terrible things but if I hadn't been helped so much, I would never have been able to deal with them. The experience's I've had have brought me to a much deeper understanding of my life and also the reason we are born to the Earth plain.

Sometimes we have to be like a child and see the Earth and Earth life as it really is. In doing that we strip away all that is false in the world and see beauty in everything, and it is beautiful. You don't have to take my word for it. Just open your heart and see the sunshine. Take away the fear and we are left with love. With love, miracles will happen. Your life will change and change forever. It will probably change in a way that you never would have imagined. But does it matter how your life changes as long as it's better for you and you're happy?

My life has changed a lot, yes it has, but I still have a very long way to go. Am I happier? Yes I am, but I haven't finished learning and growing yet. After all, I'm not perfect. I make mistakes the same as everyone else does. But it's learning to get over it and letting go that pushes me forward. So I lay in front of you the first part of my life. To bring hope and reassurance, to give you laughter and make your heart glow as you ride the roller coaster of my experience.

Chapter One
My Garden

The sky was so big; it stretched right over my house. The wind ruffled my hair and I was on my own again... well apart from the ants that were running all over the dirt. I didn't mean to hurt them, I just wanted to see how they all came out of their house together when I poked the sticks in the holes. As I watched them running around, it never occurred to me that they were angry and upset. I could feel someone standing behind me watching as well, but when I turned around there was no-one there.

The leaves on my tree, in the garden, were rustling and the wind was getting stronger. I took a long deep breath and felt the wind rushing into my nose, nearly taking my breath away. It felt like the wind was alive and pushing me around playfully, waiting for me to chase it away. I looked to the kitchen door but there was no sign of Mum. Mum was probably cooking lunch or ironing.

I loved our garden, it was huge and always full of colour and perfume from the many flowers that Mum had grown. Mum loved gardening and there were three or four large flower beds and a big rockery built up around the trunk of a large tree. Mum also made gnomes for our garden by pouring liquid concrete into rubber moulds. When they had hardened, Mum would peel the moulds off and paint them in bright colours, then place them around the rockery. You only had to look at the flowers to know what season we were in. it was beautiful all year round. Dad had made a swing for me out of some thick rope and he threw it over a low branch of the tree. This made me very happy as I sat swinging on it over the rockery. Next to our garden was another big garden belonging to the lady who lived upstairs. Her name was Mrs Langley. She was really old and walked funny. She loved the great big mop head chrysanthemums. Her garden was full of them; they were golden yellow, white, rusty red and pink. They were beautiful and so big. When I stood next to them they came right up to my waist, they smelt lovely. Right at the end of her garden was a narrow secluded bit. Mrs Langley let me go and sit quietly there, as long as I didn't disturb her flowers or go into her greenhouse. It was lovely up there, the grass was long and soft and I sat there making daisy chains or reading. There were lots of dandelions as well and I remember my Mum and Dad saying they make you wet the bed. Well I did that anyway, so it didn't matter if I picked them. The bright yellow flowers made me think of the warm sunshine. I just knew that there were fairies in that bit of the garden. When I sat there, I always felt warm and happy, even if it was a cold, windy day. To the right of that there was a garden belonging to a man and woman that were also very old and they lived in the top flat. It was really untidy and everything looked dead. But there were grasshoppers all over the place and, when no-one was looking, I used to go into their garden and try to catch them. Mum didn't like the man and woman and I would hear Mum shouting at them and the old lady would shout back. Dad would keep out of the way when this happened. I was always in the garden unless it was pouring, but if it was only raining a little bit then Mum would let me put on my red wellingtons and I would have my umbrella up and I would sit on the steps outside the back door. One day I was swinging in the garden and the sun was out but it was getting very cloudy. I could hear the rumbling of thunder all around me, but it didn't frighten me because Mum and Dad told me that it was just God moving his furniture. The clouds were getting bigger, just like bubbling mountains and I was really happy. I sang my favourite song, *Somewhere over the rainbow*. I sat there thinking that I wished I had someone to play with. Dad would play with me lots but sometimes I didn't see much of him because he worked for the Post Office and had to get up really early. Other times he worked at night and slept in the daytime. Mum liked colouring pictures with me and she would read me stories. But there were no other children who lived in the big house for me to play with, and I would feel very sad because I felt alone.

Around the side of our house, there were big concrete steps and they went down into a huge dark cellar that went under the house. Dad used to keep his motorbike down there and sometimes I went down there but I never stayed long. It was very cold and very dark, and I always got a really horrid feeling when I had to go down there to call Dad. I always felt that there was someone watching me and I didn't like it. I used to get the same feeling at night when I was in my bedroom, so, if I had to get up at night, I would run as fast as I could through the little bit of darkness into the living room. I didn't even like walking along the passageway but I knew that I just had to get through that little bit of darkness before the living room. Dad had a small fish aquarium in the passage, but it didn't give out much light. Mum would send me back to bed, but if she had gone out Dad would let me stay up until I fell asleep on the sofa. I used to remember being carried back in his arms to bed and then, when he had gone out of the room, I use to screw up my eyes so tight and curl up like a ball and somehow drift off to sleep. Sometimes I would have the most wonderful dreams; I would dream that I was flying out of the front door and up into the sky. I would be flying around my garden in the sunshine, or in the park over the road. Sometimes it would be snowing in my dreams and that was lovely. I also had lots of bad dreams. I would dream I was floating up against the ceiling and I couldn't get back to my bed. I would dream that I was trying to run out of our house with something chasing me. But the most horrible dream that I kept having was I was being tickled and I was paralysed and I couldn't get away. All of those nasty dreams gave me the really horrible feeling in my tummy and I would wake up screaming out and crying. Then Mum and Dad would come running into my bedroom to calm me down. A lot of the time they would take me into their bed with them and then I would feel safe and warm again. Sometimes when I was in my bed trying to sleep, I would feel somebody gently sitting on the end of my bed and I would open my eyes and there was no-one there. I just thought that I had been dreaming but then I would realise that I hadn't been in bed for very long and not yet been asleep. Somehow I got used to the feeling of people sitting on my bed. It made me feel all soft and warm inside. I was also aware of the feeling of cats and dogs moving on my bed. I would feel them moving round and round in a circle just like our dog Sindy did before she went to sleep.

One night I woke up and it was very dark and the house was very quiet. I could hear the wind whistling around the windows, and then I heard the gentle tapping of rain on the glass. I loved listening to that sound, and I stayed awake for quite a while. Suddenly I became aware of movement in my bedroom and out of the side of my eye I could see sparkles of light. I thought I heard my name being called and I looked around but I couldn't see anyone. I started to feel very frightened but then on the wall, up by the ceiling, appeared the most beautiful lights. There were three or four lights moving around and they were pink, green and blue. They were moving around making patterns in the dark and I watched them with wonder. With the sound of the wind, the rain and the beautiful lights, I drifted off into a beautiful sleep.

Chapter 2
David

The next morning, I could see the sun shining through the curtains and I hurried out of my bed. I looked out of the window and everything was sparkly clean. There was a huge puddle on the path that reflected the morning sky, and everything was dripping wet. At breakfast I told Mum about how I thought that, during the night, there was someone in my bedroom and I mentioned the pretty lights on the wall. Mum said that I was probably imagining it or simply dreaming, but I knew that it was real.

After we had eaten our breakfast, I asked Mum if I could play in the garden and she said yes. So I put on my wellingtons and went outside. The air smelt so different, it smelt clean and fresh, just like Mum's washing did when I helped her bring it in from the line.

I found the huge puddle and I jumped up and down in it, splashing water everywhere. It was great fun. After that I ran around and got my boots muddy and I made footprints on the steps by the back door. I heard the back door open and looked up expecting to see Mum or Dad, but standing there was a boy and he was laughing at me. He looked about the same age as me and I asked him what his name was. He said his name was David and he said that he had come to play with me. With that, we both ran around the garden splashing in the puddles. I asked him where his Mum was as I hadn't seen anyone with him. He said that his Mum was in my house.

David came to play with me more and more and I thought that his Mum and my Mum must be very good friends because he was with me nearly every day.

I had a baby brother and his name was Colin. He was a chubby little thing with lots of curly brown hair. He used to cry a lot but when he smiled his whole face lit up. Mum would put his pram out in the garden and I would rock his pram until he fell asleep. Sometimes his little cheeks would get very red and he would start crying, so I would put his dummy in his mouth and David and I would sing to him.

One day, when we were having dinner, I heard a tap on the window. It was David outside, so I pushed my plate away and went to get down from the table. But Mum told me off because I hadn't finished my dinner. So I had to sit there until I had eaten it all up. I could see David jumping up and down beckoning me, so as soon as I had finished my plate I jumped down and ran outside. Up by my Dad's shed, David was crouching on the ground looking at something. It was the biggest beetle that I had ever seen. It had big dark pincers and was very black and shiny. I placed a piece of stick in front of the beetle and watched the beetle climb over it. We were out there playing with the beetle for quite some time. David and I often used to go out hunting for different bugs and stuff. There was so much to do and so many places to hide in our garden, it was wonderful.

Sometimes I had to stay inside a lot because I wasn't well. I used to get one illness after another and my Mum was always taking me to the doctor's. But when I couldn't go out, David would come round and play with me. We would play pretending games and picture cards. He would tell me wonderful fairy tales and stories about animals that could talk. He could make lights appear on the wall and he told me it was magic. Sometimes David would pop in when it was my bedtime, and we would play. He would tell me if he heard my Mum or Dad coming towards my bedroom and he would hide so they didn't see him, then he would come out and we would play again. When I started to get tired he would sit on my bed until I fell asleep. I always felt happy when he was around and I never felt frightened of the dark. When we playing we use to talk about God. David said that God was everywhere because he was like magic. He said that God made everybody happy and kept everybody warm inside. I told him that God must be in my garden because I always felt happy and warm when I was out there. David said that God looked after everything and made all the flowers grow and all the birds sing

I said *"What about the horrible wiggly worms?"*

"Yes, those as well." he said.

One evening, when we were playing together, I asked David if he would like to stay for dinner. He said that would be lovely, so I ran into the kitchen and asked Mum if that was ok. Mum looked at me in a strange way and smiled. She said, *"Yes that's fine."* So at dinner time, when she called for me, David and I ran into the kitchen and sat down and waited. Mum brought my dinner to the table and then called Dad for his dinner, and then she put hers on the table as well. Then Dad came in and he and Mum started eating. *"What about David's dinner?"* I asked. Mum, told me to get on with my meal. I crossed my arms and said I wouldn't eat mine unless David had some as well. David just sat there without saying anything. I think he felt a bit sad and that made me cry, so Mum said, *"Ok I'll dish up some dinner for you friend."* I saw Mum and Dad smile at each other. As soon as David received his dinner I started eating mine. When I had finished my dinner, David and I went into the sitting room. We got my pencils out and started colouring pictures. I told David that I still felt a bit upset because Mum hadn't given him any food. He said that he didn't think that Mum and Dad could see him. This made me laugh and I told him that he was being silly. But then he said that I could see things that they couldn't, like the lights on my wall in the bedroom at night. He said that he didn't think that Mum and Dad could see the beautiful energy around the flowers and the trees. I was puzzled, so I asked him what he meant. He took a piece of my paper and drew a picture of a bright red flower. He coloured it in and then around the flower he did some more colouring. He coloured a golden pink mist all around it. David told me that the golden mist was the flower's energy. He then drew a picture of a tree and the put the same mist around the tree. He said that he could see this mist around all things, even me. So then I asked him what that had got to do with Mum and Dad not seeing him. He grinned at me and said that he was energy like the pretty colours around the flowers. Then he did something that really made me feel funny in my tummy. He stood up and told me to watch what he did. He walked through the door and walked back again. I was so surprised I didn't know what to say. David said that he was brought to me by an angel. He said that one day, when I was out in the garden, I had been sad because of having no-one to play with. He said that had made the angel feel sad for me, so the angel came and found him and told him that I needed a special friend. David had been watching me with the angel the day I had made the ants run out of their home. I felt so happy when he told me that. I had always known that angels were real. Even though I had never seen them, something in my heart told me that it was true.

Chapter 3
School

Mum and Dad didn't mind me talking about David, and Mum even got use to me waiting at the table for him before I started my dinner. One morning Mum said to me that I was going to start school and not to worry because I would make lots of friends. I felt a bit nervous at the thought of going to school but Mum and Dad assured me that everything would be fine.

One sunny Tuesday morning, Dad woke me up and told me to hurry into the kitchen and have breakfast. I felt very excited as Mum got me dressed in my brand new school uniform. I had on a grey pinafore dress, white blouse, shiny new shoes, and a bright red cardigan, that Mum had knitted for me. Mum put my brother in his pushchair and we all trundled out of the front door. It was the longest walked that I had ever done. All through the back streets into roads I had never been before and up a very big hill, then just as I felt I had walk far enough, we crossed a main road and I could see the school at the bottom of the next hill. As we walked into the school entrance there were lots of other children going in. we stood in a great big playground until a large lady blew a whistle. She had a smiley face, and short brown curly hair. Then she started to call out children's names. Some children started crying and I held my Mum's hand tightly. I waited with her and then the large lady called out my name. I looked at Mum and Dad and saw that Mum was wiping her eye. Dad said that she had something in it. He walked me up to the large lady with the smiley face and she took me with the other children into the school.

It was very strange sitting in a huge classroom with lots of other children. The only time I remember seeing so many children at once was when Mum and Dad took me to see Father Christmas at a big store in Croydon. In the classroom there were lots of pictures on the wall, and we had large boxes of crayons on the tables. Our teacher was the lady that I saw in the playground. She told us her name was Mrs White and said we were all her new students and she would help us to learn how to read and write. She told us that we were starting a big new adventure in our lives. She would teach us about so many things, and if we didn't understand anything we must put our hand up and wait for her to say our name, then we could ask our question. Later that morning, after colouring some shapes in, Mrs White said it was playtime and she took us out into the big playground. All the other children were there, running around, playing and shouting. Some were sitting down: others were walking along a wall trying to balance. It was wonderful. I was never allowed to run around shouting out loud, so I ran all over the place shouting my head off. A boy was running close to me and we nearly fell over each other. Laughing, we started running around together and shouting. Then we heard the whistle being blown. Everybody was told to stand still but my heart was jumping so hard in my chest that I was sure it was making me move. We were told to line up and the teachers would come and get us. I stood in line and then my new friend stood next to me. His face was all red, just like my baby brother's when he was crying. But my friend wasn't crying, he was grinning from ear to ear. I found out his name was Paul and he was also in the same class as me. At the end of the day the teacher told us to go and get our coats and wait in the corridor. Then the teacher walked us out into the playground and Mum and all the other Mums and Dads were there waiting to take us home. As we walked home, I told Mum all about school and my new friend Paul. We stopped at a sweetshop on the way home and Mum bought me and my brother a lollipop each.

When I got home I got changed and went out into the garden. David appeared and whilst we played I told him all about my new school. I told him how Mrs White said we were all starting a big new adventure. David laughed and said that all life was an adventure because we never knew what was coming.

One day at school, I was out in the playground with Paul and two more friends that we had made, and something made me look up at the sky. The sky was deep blue, just like the little forget-me-not flowers that were in my garden. The air was a little bit cold, but there, as clear as it could be, was the moon! *I couldn't believe my eyes.* The moon wasn't supposed to come out in the daytime! It was supposed to wait until the sun had gone to bed, but there it was. Right up above me like a big white balloon. I showed my friends and then we lay down on the ground just looking at the moon. It was like magic, and I was aware that as I was looking at it, all the noise of the children seemed to fade away. It was just me, the moon and the big blue sky. As I laid there I noticed there were little specks of light within the blue sky. They were moving really fast and when I relaxed my eyes I could see even more of them. The moon started to look different as well. It looked a lot closer and I could see a mist around it. The mist turned a beautiful golden colour with pink around the edges. All of a sudden the whistle blew and made me jump. As I stood up I felt a bit dizzy and wobbled. I went to line up and as I was waiting I looked back at the moon, but the beautiful mist had disappeared and so had the specks of light in the sky. When I next saw David I told him about seeing the moon and the specks in the sky. He said that was brilliant because now I knew what he meant when he said everything was made of energy. He told me that everything vibrates at different frequencies and God made it like this because it made room for everything in the universe.

I was getting on really well at school and making lots of friends and when I got home from school I would tell David about my day. One day when I got home from school Mum told me that she had a special surprise for me and Colin. She told us that we were going to have a baby brother or sister in a couple of weeks' time. It happened one sunny day in July. Colin and I were playing in the garden and Dad came out of the back door. He called us both in and told us to walk quietly into their bedroom. There was Mum sitting up in bed holding a tiny baby. Mum said we had got a little sister and her name was Denise. Denise was really small and she was wrapped in a white blanket which Mum had made. Denise had hardly any hair at all, but we all thought that she was lovely.

One day David and I were playing in the garden when he told me that he would be going away for a while. He said he had to go to a place of learning and he would meet lots of different teachers and they would teach him lots of different things. He said it was like a big school but the building was white and there were lots of pillars around the edge of it. It sounded like the buildings that my teacher had told us about it in ancient Greece. David said that inside it was beautiful, and there were thousands of books with lovely pictures in them. He said that as I had more friends now, he knew I wouldn't mind if I didn't see so much of him, as I wouldn't be so lonely anymore. He told me that he had made some new friends as well and he was very excited about this. I think I must have known that David was going away because since I had been going to school, I noticed that he had not been coming over every day. Sometimes it had been a whole week since I had seen him. I didn't mind because I really enjoyed all the different things he told me about, and if he was going to school he could tell me more.

Chapter 4
Terrified

As the weeks went on, I seemed to catch cold after cold and also many other illnesses. Whenever I was ill or in bed, I would always feel someone sitting on the end of my bed. I couldn't see anyone there and I never knew who it was. But it didn't worry me because I knew that they were looking after me just like Mum and Dad did...

One night I woke up when it was really dark and I couldn't get back to sleep so I picked up one of my favourite books and started to read. It was very quiet in the house and I knew that everyone else was probably fast asleep. After a while I started to feel sleepy again, so I put the book on the floor and got out of bed to get my best doll to sleep with. I had a playhouse in my bedroom, up by the windows. I went in there to get my doll. She was beautiful; she was a big doll that had curly golden hair. She had big blue eyes that closed when I laid her down. Her dress was pale blue and all frilly around the edge. I picked her up and took her into my bed with me. I always went to sleep on my tummy so I turned over and had my doll on the left between me and the wall. I was just about to close my eyes when I was aware of a tingling feeling coming all over my body. It got stronger and stronger and it made all my hair on my head stand up. I was aware of someone standing by my bed but I didn't dare turn over to look. It felt like all the hair from my toes to my head were all standing on end. I felt my stomach tighten up like a hard ball and

I could feel tears in my eyes. I was absolutely terrified. I squeezed my eyes shut as tight as I could, hardly daring to take a breath. I somehow managed to go off to sleep because when I opened my eyes the sun was streaming through the curtains and I could hear Mum and Dad in the kitchen. I got up, forgetting all about the frightening night that I had just had and I got dressed. Then I went to get my doll but it wasn't in my bed so I looked on the floor in case it had fallen off in the night. It wasn't there so I felt all down by the wall to see if it was stuck there, but it wasn't there either. I searched everywhere, even back in the playhouse, but it was nowhere to be seen. I went into the kitchen and asked Mum and Dad if they had taken my doll. They both said no. I asked Colin and he said no as well. I didn't think Colin would have taken it because he had his action men and he didn't like my dolls. As for Denise, well she was just a baby. She couldn't even walk by herself, let alone carry a doll that was as big as she was. As I was puzzling over this, I suddenly remembered my frightening night. My tummy had a horrible feeling in it again. I now knew what had happened. Whoever or whatever had been in my bedroom had taken my doll. Once I realised that, I felt really sick and started to shake. Mum asked me if I was ok and I said I didn't feel well so she felt my forehead and she said to Dad that I felt all sweaty. Mum kept me off school again, saying that if I wasn't better the next day she would take me to the doctor's. After that night I felt really frightened about sleeping in my bedroom in the dark. Dad bought me a pretty lamp and put it up for me. But there wasn't a week that went by that I didn't wake up Mum and Dad screaming because of nightmares. I would dream that I was being chased by my doll, and sometimes I would dream that I was being held down by my doll and it tickled me until I screamed for it to stop. I would see the patterns of flowers on the curtains change into dolls faces and also the faces of clowns. My Mum and Dad got rid of all my dolls. I couldn't even see them in toy shops without it affecting me badly. Even my wonderful flying dreams I always had turned really nightmarish, and all this affected my everyday life. I was off of school more and more and I became very quiet and nervous. I would shake terribly and my life felt just horrible. Mum was really worried about me and took me to see our doctor. While Mum was talking to him, I played with the Lego bricks in the waiting room until Mum came out. I found out, many years later, that the doctor said that I was picking up on the tension between Mum and Dad. They tended to argue a lot but never in front of us children. I used to hear them in the bedroom arguing, but I know it was the night that my doll had vanished that my problems started.

Chapter 5
Imagination

As I was off school so much, I was falling behind with my learning so Mum and Dad decided to bring in a private tutor. His name was Martin and he would teach me Maths and English. But when I was in bed ill, if I wasn't really bad he would read to me. I had lots of story books and one of my favourites was a big story book all about animals that lived in the woods. The book had a lovely picture on it of tall, graceful trees and delicate blue and yellow flowers in the grass. There was a deer and a couple of rabbits as well, and I used to look at that picture when I was sad and imagine that I was there. I'd close my eyes and, as if by magic, was there. I would walk through the trees looking at the pretty flowers and feeling the soft grass beneath my feet. The trees would be extremely tall and I could never see the tops. I would hear the birds singing and feel the wind on my face. The wind would blow my hair up and I could feel the energy of everything there. There were also lots of rabbits and other animals everywhere. It was lovely. It would feel like the woods were magical because sometimes there would be surprises in the woods, like people who would walk up and talk to me. Even the animals would seem to talk to me, but not out loud, just in my mind. It was magical, as though I had somehow come out of my house and straight into the picture. Nearly every time I did this, sooner or later I would feel a sudden jolt and I would open my eyes to find myself back in my room. I always felt happier afterwards as well. I was thinking about this one day and a little voice in my head said, that if I used my imagination to help me feel better, I could use it to help when I was frightened. So the next night, when Mum put me to bed and I lay there trying to sleep, I remembered the patterns on the curtains that frightened me. I looked at them and waited. Sure enough the flowers started to change. Once again I could feel that horrible feeling in my tummy. I forced myself to carry on looking and when the patterns changed into the faces, I imagined putting flower pots over their heads, then I would imaging throwing balls at them and knocking them off, just like on the coconut shy. Once I had done that, I would turn over and go straight to sleep. I did this for maybe a week or so and then, as time went by, I would think *"Oh I can't be bothered to do that tonight,"* and I would go straight to sleep without any worries. I was also able to use my imagination to help me with any noises at night. Our house was very old and I would hear lots of creaking noises which often frightened me. When I heard these noises, I would imagine lots of little mice having parties and dancing. This was really easy because even though we had a cat called Fluffy, we still had mice. Mum hated the mice which was why she bought Fluffy. But I loved them because I loved all animals and they were so cute. I would often see one sitting on top of the big radio in the kitchen. I wouldn't tell Mum or Dad, I would just sit there watching the mouse watching us.

Mum started to get worried about our dog Sindy, she had been really ill and Mum and Dad had taken her to the vet's quite a lot in those few weeks. One day Mum told us that Sindy had been really ill and the vet said that it wasn't fair to let her be in pain and there was no more that he could do for her. She kept being sick and wasn't eating properly, so Mum had agreed to the vet giving her an injection to put her to sleep. We all felt upset, but the next day Mum was brushing my hair while I sat on the chair in the kitchen, and through the window I saw Sindy sitting on the grass in the sun. I told Mum I had just seen her but Mum said I must have imagined it. I knew I hadn't and felt vindicated later when I heard Mum telling my Gran on the telephone about it, and Mum told Gran that she had seen Sindy in her bedroom laying on the chair. *I knew I had seen her* and it really puzzled me that whenever I told Mum I had seen things or felt things she didn't believe me. After that I tended to keep things that I heard or saw to myself. Gradually my nights became better and better, and I began to sleep more easily. Then Mum had a change around in the house and I was moved to the large bedroom in the front of the house. I then shared this bedroom with Colin and Denise. That was the end of my scary nights altogether, because after we had been put to bed we used to get up again and play together. We'd chase each other around the bedroom throwing pillows around, trying to be really quiet. Sometimes Mum and Dad would catch us and tell us off. But most of the time we managed to jump back in bed just before Mum or Dad came in.

Chapter 6
A new beginning

One day Mum called us all into the living room and said she had something important to tell us. She told us that Dad wasn't going to live with us anymore. She told us that things had become difficult between them as they argued most of the time. She said that Dad and her had decided that it was for the best, and Dad would still see us but live somewhere else. Mum said it would be like Dad was working nights all the time, so it wouldn't be as bad as it sounded. I was ok with this and it didn't seem to affect me a lot. As long as I would still see Dad I didn't mind. Colin was upset and so was Denise and Mum cuddled us all. Gradually we got used to this new arrangement and we always looked forward to Dad coming over. He was always there for tea on a Tuesday and sometimes he met us from school. What we didn't miss was the arguing that went on and the slamming of the doors. . .

A few months later, Mum told us that we had to move because the people who owned our house had sold it and it was going to be demolished. A block of flats was going to be built on the land. Mum said that our house was really old and that some of our neighbours had already moved out. We didn't want to leave and the thought of leaving our lovely home and the huge garden really upset me. I think I cried for weeks. *Why couldn't we stay there?* It really made us sad. Mum told me that she had a choice of three houses to live in and if she didn't choose one, we would have nowhere to live. The first offer was a flat over a shop, and Mum wasn't impressed at all. The flat was very dark and pokey. After living in such a big house, this felt like a prison and there was hardly any room for our furniture. The next was a flat where a sitting room and kitchen was on one floor, and then we had to walk upstairs past someone else's front door to get to the bathroom and the bedrooms. Mum said absolutely not. There was no way she was going to let us walk past someone else's front door in our nightclothes.

The last and final offer was the most suitable. It was in another town called Croydon, and it was a three bedroomed terraced house, it was up a hill named Harrisons Rise. Mum would have her own bedroom, Colin would have his own bedroom and I would share with Denise. It was perfect for us. It had a garden that wasn't very big but it had a tree in it. We went to see the house in November and the last of the leaves were ready to fall. The ones on the ground were all crispy. Colin, Denise and I ran around the garden kicking the leaves in the air. The Earth smelt musky and there was a hint of smoke in the air, it came from one of the gardens up the hill. Someone had started a bonfire there. We said to Mum that we liked this house and we didn't mind moving there. Mum laughed and said that she had already said yes to this offer.

Our home was in chaos, there were boxes and crates everywhere. But we were very excited. Mum went into our bedroom and with some help from the removal men, started to pull the furniture out. There was an old bed that had been standing up on its side with a sheet over it. Mum and Dad had put it there to block up a dirty old fireplace when they changed our bedrooms around. The fireplace had never been used since we moved there. When the bed was pulled away from the wall Mum shouted out *"Look what we've found!"* I looked up and in Mum's hand there was the doll that had gone missing a few years before.

It was filthy and covered with soot. Mum asked me if I wanted it but it bought back a feeling so horrible that I could even go near it. I felt tears coming into my eyes as I shouted at Mum to throw the doll away. I never knew how that doll came to be there and seeing it again brought that frightening night right back to me.

We moved on a very cold morning in December. We found a takeaway shop just around the corner and we sat on boxes in our new living room to eat fish and chips out of the newspaper wrapping. It was wonderful, and just when I didn't think things could get any better it started to snow and Dad walked in.

It seemed to take weeks before everything was sorted out. Mum had bought Denise and me bunk beds. I had the bottom one and Denise slept on the top. As I laid there looking up, I could see the edge of Denise's pillow. Just as Denise drifted off to sleep that night, I grabbed her pillow and pulled it out from underneath her. We were both in fits of giggles and that trick went on for many a night. Colin loved his new bedroom even though it was tiny. The cheeky boy stuck a large *No Entry* sign on the door and wrote *PRIVATE NO GIRLS* in big letters underneath it.

One day when Mum was in the kitchen and I was watching television, I heard the front door knocker go. I went to the door and opened it to find there was no-one there. So I shut the door and went back to watching television. It knocked again and I went to answer it. There was no-one there again. I started to get the strange feeling in my stomach that I used feel when I was scared. I went in the kitchen and told Mum. It was probably my imagination she said. Then it went again and this time Mum heard it as well. She went to the door and then she came back to me and said it's probably children mucking around. Then the knocker went mad and we both ran to the door and opened it, but no-one was there. This time we waited right behind the door. "*We'll catch the little buggers,*" said Mum. Suddenly we saw a shadow of something moving down the outside of the door. Mum flung the door open to see my brother hanging out of his bedroom window with a length of string and a coat hanger tied to the end. It was Colin hooking the letterbox with the hanger. I burst out laughing and Mum started shouting at him and then went running up the stairs to tell him off. I went back to the living room to carry on watching telly. Mum came down and went back into the kitchen and Colin came down grinning from ear to ear. Colin drove us mad many times with this trick until Mum finally had enough and nailed his window shut.

Chapter 7
Mum

The winter seemed to last forever and what made it worse, was that March and April seemed colder than December. The condensation on our bedroom windows turned to ice through the night and I slept with more clothes on during the night than I wore during the day. I had moved up to senior school and Colin and Denise were in the juniors. Dad still came over every Tuesday and Mum had a boyfriend called Robert, who she had met at work. Life became a very busy world for all of us... new friends, lots of work, and Mum never minded who we invited back for dinner. Our home was always full of noise, music, laughter and tears. We had a new puppy that we named Sandy; he was a white and sandy coloured mongrel. He was a cross between a Wire Haired Terrier and a Jack Russell. He had a little white scruffy beard, and was totally mad. Mum and Robert brought him home from the pub one day. A man brought him in and said that if he couldn't find a home for him he would have to have him put to sleep. Mum had always been an animal lover and she took one look at him and was hooked.

We used to go and visit our grandparents regularly. They were as different as chalk and cheese. Granddad Hyne (Alf) was my Dad's Dad. He was very happy and always helping his neighbours out. He would play games with us and would always be smiling. Nanny Hyne (Gladys) was really cuddly; she always had her apron on and made us cakes every time we came over. Pop was my

Mum's Dad; his name was John Faulker. We didn't see much of him and when we did we were always very quiet. It wasn't that we didn't like him, we didn't really know him. He was very Victorian and children were meant to be seen and not heard. Although I'm sure he cared for us, he never showed it as far as I remember. My gran, (Lillian, or Lill as she liked to be known) was very different. She bought us sweets and had a wicked sense of humour. We could tell she always enjoyed our company.

Gran and Pop lived in the basement flat of a big house in a town called Anerley. It was quite dark in their home and there was nearly always a light on. To get to their toilet you had to walk through their bedroom, which was at the front of their house, and go up two steps into the bathroom. There was something about their bedroom that I really didn't like. It was always in darkness because there was no window in it, and it smelt very musky. If I wanted to go to the toilet, I would put it off for as long as I could, then I would run through the bedroom as fast as I could to the bathroom, and when I had finished I would run back again. I wouldn't stay in there for one second too long, and when I was back in the hallway I would always look back into the darkness of the bedroom. It would never have surprised me if I saw a ghost following me. One night after visiting them, I told Mum how I felt every time I was going through their bedroom. To my amazement, instead of Mum saying it was my imagination, she totally agreed with what I said. Mum said she had never had a good feeling about that room and she also ran to the bathroom and back again.

Then Mum started to tell me other things. She told me that when we lived in the other house, there was that day when I had told her I had seen our dead dog Sindy. Well, Mum had also seen her about five minutes before I had. I then remembered the phone call between Mum and Gran. I asked her why she had said it was my imagination when she had seen Sindy with her own eyes. Mum said that she didn't want these things to frighten me as I had become such a nervous child. Mum said that both Dad and she had seen spirits in that house. Dad had seen a monk stepping through the wardrobe door; Mum said that Dad had gone as white as a sheet. Mum had seen a nun looking over Denise one night as she slept in her cot. She also heard the voices of people who weren't there. She was really frightened of all the things she had seen, so she thought the best thing that she could do for me, was to tell me the things that I had seen were just my imagination. Mum then went on to say that when Dad and she were dating as teenagers, they were over at some lakes with another couple and they had taken a walk that led away from the lakes onto land that was rough and overgrown. All of a sudden there was a ghost, wearing a pointed hood over its face, flying towards them and it was screaming at them. Mum and Dad ran away along with the other couple and they were all absolutely terrified. This dreadful experience had led to Mum and Dad being terrified of spirits from that day on.

Well, after that I totally understood why Mum did what she did. Then Mum said that in the house that we lived in now, she had seen the spirit of an old lady walking up the stairs, so she refused to walk along the top passage without the top light on. Mum also told me that she could feel herself coming out of her body at night. She would find herself up at the ceiling looking down at herself in bed, it totally terrified her.

So there you are! I got the whole truth all in one evening, and guess what it did? *It frightened the life out of me.* From that evening I would turn the light on at the top passage before I would go into the toilet. I would never look downstairs in case I saw the old lady, and as for coming out of my body when I was asleep, I never slept on my back in case it happened to me. I had forgotten about my wonderful flying dreams that I used to have as a small child. My invisible friend David and all of my wonderful experiences, had been buried deeply inside, under layers and layers of fear.

Chapter 8
Tree spirits

Mum always made sure that we had two decent holidays a year; we would always go when it was cheapest and it didn't seem to matter if we had to take time off school. It was doing that or not going at all. Mum worked so hard to raise the three of us. She had a full time job and looked permanently tired. So not to be able to go away was out of the question.

One June, we went down to a beautiful caravan park in Dorset. It was very big and it had its own beach by a beautiful harbour. The caravans were wonderful and we were always excited to stay in them. The caravans in those days did not have running water or toilets/showers in them. But it didn't matter. It just made them more exciting for us. We would go along to the club in the evenings and drink pop and dance or play in the amusement arcades. The penny arcades they were called and that's exactly what they cost to play, 1 penny.

One night, we had been to the club and on the way back we all rushed to the toilet block before we went into the caravan. We had torches so we could see in the dark as it was about 11o'clock. All around the toilet block were streetlights but as you got further away there weren't so many. The paths that ran along the side of the streetlights were lined with trees. As you went into the toilet blocks, they were well lit, so much that they were a beacon of light to all the moths, crane flies and bugs in Dorset. I didn't mind though, the crane flies especially fascinated me with their long spindly legs and their delicate wings... I would catch them as gently as I could and then watch them walk all over my hands. I never understood all the other girls and women who screamed and made such a fuss when they flew near them.

The moths were all different sizes and they glistened with silver dust when the light caught their wings. I never held them though. I thought that if the silver dust came off of them, they wouldn't be able to fly, and that would be awful.

As for the bugs, they all looked black or brown from a distance, but when you got really close to them they had beautiful shimmery colours on them. Purple, emerald green, sapphire blue...

I would always be the last one back to the caravan and that night was no exception. Mum locked the caravan door and we all went to bed. In the night I was having a dream that I was running around looking for the toilet when I suddenly woke up, realising that I really did need to go. I wrapped myself in my coat and put my shoes on. Taking my torch with me, I crept out of the caravan and started on my way to the toilet block. The night was cool and very clear with a bright full moon. Only a few of the street lights were on and no other lights were on apart from the toilet block in the distance. I was really tired and the lights in the toilet block were way too bright for my sleepy eyes. I went to the toilet then washed my hands and started my walk back. I was shining my torch all over the place, making sure that I didn't shine it in other people's caravan windows. I didn't mind being out in the dark on my own because it was so still and quiet. As I was walking back something made me turn around. I looked at the trees that lined the path and every tree had a face in the leaves. I turned away and looked in front and all the trees ahead of me had big faces as well, I was really frightened. I ran as fast as I could with my eyes down, forgetting to use my torch and stumbling along the way. I got to our caravan, jumped inside and locked the door. I didn't even take my coat and shoes off; I just jumped straight into bed and shut my eyes tight. The next morning was bright and sunny, and as I helped Mum cook breakfast, I made a promise that I wouldn't tell anyone what had happened that night, and I would put a bucket under my bed so I wouldn't have to go outside at night anymore. Needless to say, I was never the last one back to the caravan after that.

Chapter 9
Pop

A few years later, my Pop became very ill. He had developed lung cancer. He had been in hospital and they had treated him with radiotherapy for his cancer, but unfortunately the treatment was unsuccessful and they couldn't do any more for him. So he came home to spend his last couple of weeks in peaceful surroundings.

Colin and Denise weren't old enough to be home at night by themselves, so I would go to my gran's house straight from school and stay overnight and travel to school from there by bus the next morning. When Mum had got Colin and Denise ready for school, she would see them off in the morning and then come over by bus. That way Gran and Pop always had someone with them. Pop's bed was made up in the living room as the bedroom was dark and dingy. Also, if Pop wanted to, he could see the television.

My Aunty June, (Mum's sister) lived a very long way away so she had to visit at the weekends.

One evening, I was watching television whilst sitting on the side of Pop's bed. I was holding his hand and Gran was in the kitchen washing up. Gran came in to pull the cloth off of the table and she looked over at Pop. Gran came to the bedside and looked closer at him. His eyes were closed and I thought that he had gone to sleep. Gran wasn't so sure because she couldn't see him breathing. She went and got a mirror out of the bathroom and came back and held it above Pop's face. She told me that Pop's breathing had been very shallow in the past few days, so using a mirror she would be able to see if he was still breathing. I sat there hardly daring to breathe myself... but there was no breath on the mirror. Pop had passed away. Gran put the mirror down and told me to go and ring Mum, and I saw Gran put a sheet over Pop's face.

I rang Mum and told her Pop had gone. She said to stay with Gran and she would get a taxi and be straight over. I went into the kitchen to tell Gran and she was standing by the sink. She wouldn't turn around but told me to go back to the other room and wait for Mum. After a short while, I heard the doorbell. I told Gran I would get the door. I opened the door expecting to see Mum but there was no-one there. As I closed the door, something made me look up and there was Pop's face. His face was rising above me, just looking at me, not smiling, just looking and floating upwards. I closed the door and went back to the living room. I didn't tell Gran what I had just seen. I just told her there was no-one there. I sat on the armchair waiting for Mum. Then the doorbell rang. I couldn't believe... the doorbell I had heard earlier, was a totally different ring to the one I had just heard. Gran's doorbell was a really harsh ring, whereas the one I heard when I saw Pop, was a ding dong.

I let Mum in and with her was Robert. He took me back to my house in the taxi. That night, as I lay in bed, I couldn't stop thinking about seeing Pop. The more I thought about it the more sure I was that he was letting me know he was ok. The next day, Mum came home for a while before going with Gran to sort out the funeral arrangements. It was a few weeks after the funeral that I told Mum what I'd seen. Mum said that he was probably letting me know that he was ok. I smiled because I knew that was right. We saw a lot more of my Gran after Pop passed away. It was very lonely for her living on her own. And sometimes when we were over there we would hear strange bangs on the cupboard door in the living room. It would normally happen after Gran had given Mum something. Mum would laugh and say *"Dad never liked you giving anything away."*

As we grew older, Mum started taking holidays abroad. The first time Mum did this, she was really scared at the thought of flying. But as the plane was taking off she saw Pop and she knew he was watching over her. From that time, whenever she went abroad she would always see Pop as she was travelling. One day she even saw him sitting outside on the wing. Knowing that Pop was still looking after her stopped her worrying and made her feel safe. Even now, over thirty years later, Mum still asks Pop to help her if she's worried, and he always does.

Chapter 10
The worst film ever

Even though I had had some really frightening experiences as a child, like most teenagers I loved a good horror film. What made me really brave was that I had long hair with a long fringe and I used to pull my fringe over my eyes so I couldn't see what was going on properly. I am very short sighted in my right eye, so that made me even braver. When I knew something nasty was going to happen in the films, I would close my good eye and watch with my bad eye. I always made sure that I would sit on the left hand side of people so they never knew. I wonder now why I put myself through it. When I think about it, I suppose that it was my way of trying to overcome the fear. It was a kind of cheating. I sat through them all, half watching and half hiding. I would tell all my friends what I'd seen and make up most of the gory bits.

One night, my Mum's friend asked me if I would like to go to the pictures with her to see a horror film. She was a horror fanatic. Mum said she didn't want to go as it wasn't her sort of film. I think the film was called *The Heretic*. I went with Mum's friend looking, forward to a good night out. In those days they always played two films, with an intermission in the middle. The film came on and I sat there thoroughly enjoying it, pulling my fringe down and closing my good eye when I had to. It was brilliant. In the intermission we went and got ice creams and waited to see what the next film was. To my absolute horror, it was a film called *The Exorcist*. I had read about this film in the papers and had heard people talking about it everywhere.

They said it was a really frightening film and lots of people had been very upset by it. Because of what I had heard, I swore that I would never go and see it. Yet there I was, sitting in the pictures with it starting in front of me. I was already frightened as the opening credits were just starting.

Well, I sat there for about five minutes watching. It was horrid; a big man who was sitting in front of me swore and walked out. I looked up and I saw a terrible face of a demon on a child and that was enough for me. I looked at my Mum's friend and I could see that she was enjoying it. So there I sat through the whole of the film, not daring to look at the screen but only looking down into my lap, with my hair pulled down over my eyes. It didn't really help though, because I could hear everything that was going on. Finally, after what seemed like a lifetime, it finished. Mum's friend said that she thought it was the best film that she had ever seen. I told her that I hated it. She said I should've told her and we could have left. But I didn't want her to think that I was a coward, which was why I didn't say anything. If only I'd known how that film was going to affect me. When we got back to my house I made a drink and sat down watching television. After a while Mum said it was late and we should go to bed. I went up to my bedroom and lay in my bed petrified.

There was no way I could sleep with the light off. I even sneaked Sandy up there to sleep on the bed with me. I kept thinking about that terrible film and not even the lamp in my bedroom made me feel better. Or the fact that Denise was asleep in the top bunk. I got out of bed and put the big light on. This I did for at least six months and even when I stayed at my boyfriend's house I slept with the light on. I was eighteen years old, worked in London, had not long got engaged to be married, and all because of that film I was still afraid of the dark. That film haunted me for a long time afterwards and needless to say, I never watched any more horror films again.

Chapter 11
Denise

Denise and I were different in so many ways. Even as a small child she was a lot more headstrong. She was tidy, I wasn't. She dressed like a tomboy and I liked girlie things. I was very placid and Denise blew her top most of the time, unless she was out with her friends. Having said that, we did love each other but I guess, like most siblings, you never say that. Mum always said it was as though Denise had a problem with being the youngest in the family. Mum also said it was as though Denise should have been an only child. I know that she never got over Mum and Dad splitting up, so maybe that had something to do with it. Denise was always very energetic and very rarely stayed still. After she left school she started training on a course to become a chef, which seemed strange as she hardly ate much. She very rarely ate a proper meal; in fact she snacked through the week seeming to fill up at the weekends. When she wasn't working, she was out with her friends and she always stayed up until the early hours of the morning even though she had to be up at six. It was almost as though she didn't have enough time to fit in everything that she wanted to do. She even started smoking cigarettes at eleven years old. One day, out of the blue, she said to Mum that she was going to die in a car crash. Mum told her not to be so silly. Two or three times that year the same conversation came up. It happened one October in 1985. Denise had gone out on a date one evening, to a restaurant in New Addington. Mum told her not to get a bus home as it would be late at night. She must get a taxi. Denise was picked up by a taxi from the restaurant and on the way home, going up a very steep winding hill, a car driven by a man who had had too much to drink, came onto the wrong side of the road and crashed into the taxi, killing the taxi driver outright and putting Denise in hospital on a life support machine. The life support machine was turned off three days later and Denise passed away.

It was a terribly sad time for all of my family but Denise was soon able to let us know that she was ok. A few days later, Mum was sitting in her armchair dozing. Mum had a vision of Denise wrapped in a blanket with her eyes closed and next to her was my Gran and Pop. It was about a week later that I went to bed late at night and I was laying there when I sensed someone by my bed. I dismissed it at first but the feeling got stronger and stronger. Then I was aware that I could hear breathing. I knew it was Denise. I know it sounds silly but I recognised her breathing. Then I began to feel very frightened, so with that, I flew out of bed and along the top passageway, down the stairs and straight into the front room, where my boyfriend was sleeping at the time. I stayed downstairs with him and crept back upstairs at about 7 o'clock. I felt so silly to be frightened. After all it was Denise, but I still couldn't overcome the fear. Just two months later, on Christmas day morning, Mum saw Denise standing behind me in the kitchen. This didn't take the sadness of what happened to her away, but it did make it easier because we knew Denise was alright.

The following May, my boyfriend and I got married. It was a lovely sunny day but very windy. We were married in Croydon parish church. The church was huge and very beautiful, and the day was perfect apart from one thing. I had five bridesmaids and Denise was supposed to be one as well. We had many photos taken and Mum had a video camera which was also used. We went to the Isle of Wight for our honeymoon. The last week in May and the following June, was as cold and wet as early spring. When we got back from our honeymoon, Mum had a wonderful story to tell us. A friend of hers, who had come to visit her, was shown the video of our wedding. Her friend June was very psychic and, as she was watching the video, she told Mum that she could see Denise standing next to the other bridesmaids, in a matching bridesmaid dress. How wonderful, Denise was there after all.

In those next twelve months, life was changing for everyone; Gary and I were married, Colin moved in with his girlfriend. Denise passed away. Mum's boyfriend, Robert, had also passed away with cancer. Mum had bought a new dog to give Sandy company. She called her Sindy. She had also met a wonderful new friend called Bill. It seemed that life was in constant motion with nothing staying still.

Chapter 12
Married life

Gary and I, moved into a two bedroomed house in Strood in Kent, and I'll always remember that first morning after we moved in. I opened the front door and the air smelt beautiful. It was so fresh and clean after the pollution of Croydon. Croydon was so busy, even in the middle of the night the traffic was always busy. But where we moved to was just like being out in the countryside. The best thing about it, was the tallest things that broke the skyline, were Rochester castle and Rochester cathedral. So different from the gigantic tower blocks that I used to see from my home back in Croydon. Gary and I were both at work. He worked as a car mechanic in Dartford and I worked on the switchboard at the Midland bank in Maidstone. We were very happy but our house seemed empty. I was always used to people popping in and out when I lived at Mum's. Mum often said her home was like a hotel, in the nicest way of course. There were always friends coming and going. With two dogs, a mynah bird, and numerous other pets, our home was buzzing with life. Gary also came from a busy home, living with his Mum and Dad, three sisters and pets galore. It was so strange to come into our home, into the peace and quiet with no-one else around. So, for my birthday, Gary gave me two gorgeous black and white kittens. They were just what we needed to cheer the place up. We named them Missy and Sparky and they were furry balls of chaos which we absolutely adored. Missy grew into a beautiful graceful cat and

Sparky developed two long fangs and a dreadful meow. He reminded us of a mad vampire. We were sure Sparky wasn't quite right in the head because he had a habit of chewing my hairbrushes. He would sit and chew on the bristles for hours. Gary and I had often spoken, before we got married, of how many children we'd have. I always liked the thought of having 4 children but I knew that I wanted to have two boys first. I fell pregnant with my first child when I was twenty-seven. I had never felt so ill for as long as I could remember. For the first four months I was hardly at work. I couldn't keep anything down apart from oranges and yogurt and the day my sickness stopped it felt like my birthday and I treated Gary and I to a steak meal with all the trimmings. Our son was born on the 30th July and we named him Richard James Knight. Of course he was beautiful and we were so proud, along with two sets of new grandparents, as well as a great grandmother and two great grandfathers. My psychic experiences stopped and my fear of sleeping in the dark had all but disappeared as my life was taken up with being a wife and a mother. Three years later on the 11th September, I gave birth to another boy who we named Glen Douglas Knight. I was over the moon as I had got my wish, having two boys. We would travel up to Croydon every three weeks or so to see Mum, and, one day when we were there, Richard was playing in Mum's front room and we called him to come and have his dinner. As Richard came into the sitting room, he asked me who the boy was in there. I got up to have a look and there was no-one else in the room. We think that Richard had seen Denise sitting there. To someone as young as Richard was, she would have indeed looked like a boy as she was very slim and wore boyish clothes. Another time, on the way home from Mum's, we were in the car and above the music on the radio, Gary and I could hear Richard talking to someone. Glen was asleep, so we asked Richard who he was talking to. He said "*my friend.*" I asked him who his friend was and he said "*Tracy, she lives up in the sky!*" Well it seemed that Richard had got an invisible friend as well. We didn't make too much of it and Richard didn't speak of her any more.

One Wednesday morning, Mum rang up. She was sad because Sandy had passed away that morning. But Mum said that a wonderful thing had happened. Sindy had helped him. Sandy needed to go out into the garden to go to the toilet. He waited by the back door, hardly able to stand and when Mum opened the back door for him he very slowly walked out into the garden. Sindy followed him and together they walked slowly down to the end of the garden. Sandy went to the toilet and they both walked slowly up to the back door to come in. both dogs walked in and Sandy lay down with Sindy next to him and he gently passed away. It was so lovely for us to know that Sindy was watching over him for as long as he needed her.

Chapter 13
There must be more to life

Richard was now going to infants' school and Glen was at playgroup, life was getting back on track. The sleep-disturbed nights had more or less ended and I was starting to feel like my old self again. It had been very exhausting looking after the boys, shopping, cooking and needing sleep. My heart went out to all the parents and especially to my Mum and Dad. At infants' school, Richard had made a friend called Thomas and he lived at the bottom of our road. We would walk up to school with Tom and his Mum and we all became good friends. I would take Tom to school with us or pick him up if she couldn't and she would do the same for me. About two years later, in the springtime, Tom's Mum had been taken into hospital with what they thought was a dreadful migraine. It turned out that she had had a brain haemorrhage. She was in hospital for about three weeks and the doctors thought she was going to come out soon. Very sadly, my friend died suddenly as another haemorrhage appeared. We were all devastated. Everyone thought that she was getting better. I cried myself to sleep the evening that I found out she had died. When I eventually drifted off to sleep I had a beautiful dream. I dreamt I was downstairs and my friend was in my living room. I was crying and it seems silly to say that I could feel every curve of her body as she comforted me. She was dressed in a lovely dark blue dress with white polka dots on. As she cuddled me it felt so real. It had to be more than a dream. When I woke up the next morning I felt so much better, as though a weight had been lifted from me. That was on the Monday and on the Friday I had more sad news. My Dad's father had passed away at the age of 84. I had been expecting granddad to pass away for quite a few months because he had been very ill with cancer, but for it to happen the same week as my friend was just so sad for me. The following week I dreamt about granddad. We were talking and he was smiling, but I can't remember what we spoke about in the dream. But I do remember that he wasn't ill anymore but looking healthier than I remembered for a long time.

Over the next six months, I dreamt about granddad regularly and in every dream he was a little younger. He then seemed to stay at about the age of forty-five. I think maybe this was the age when my granddad felt happiest. At Glen's playgroup, I got talking to a woman about my age; she also had one of her children there as well. We became good friends and for a few years her family and my family became very close. She told me that she could see spirits and she had always seen them. She went on to tell me, that before she had fallen pregnant with her first child, she was resting on the sofa and her Dad appeared to her carrying a baby in his arms. The baby had got ginger hair. One month later she fell pregnant and when the baby was born he had indeed got ginger hair. We spoke about a lot to do with spirit, of ghosts as we would call them. I realised, as much as I was afraid of it, I wanted to know more. I noticed that when I was at home during the day, I kept thinking I could see someone out of the corner of my eye. Also I found that I seemed to be thinking more and more of my sister.

One day I was in the news agents and I saw a small magazine for sale. It was called *Two Worlds* and it had a picture of a Native American Indian on the front of it. Inside there were many stories of healing and people having spiritual experiences. It also spoke of mediums, spiritual churches and centres. I found it so interesting that I placed a monthly order for it. In the back of the magazine there were mediums that were advertising to give people readings. I decided that I would write to a medium to see if they could give me a message from Denise. I picked a lady who lived down on the south coast. It said in her advertisement, to send a photo or a piece of hair, along with a cheque for £12. I decided to send a piece of my hair as I thought it more personal. I sent it if with my name, address and the cheque and waited patiently. I was talking to my Mum on the phone that evening about writing to the medium, and Mum said to me. *"What is it you're after?"* I told her *"Well I'm married with two lovely boys but there's got to be more to life than this."* Gary, Richard, Glen and I were quite happy but that wasn't enough. There was something inside me stirring but I didn't know what it was. Just over a week later, I had a letter back from the medium I had written to. She told me that she had a woman with her who had short, grey curly hair. She had a cuddly stature and a lovely smile. Also there was a younger woman with sparkling laughter and short brown hair who had passed suddenly. Apart from that she couldn't tell me much more. Well the first description sounded like my Nan but I couldn't be sure. The second description sounded very much like my friend who died with the brain haemorrhage. The medium didn't give much else and what she did give was very vague. I did feel very disappointed. Nevertheless I wrote back thanking her but asking if she had received any information about Denise. I received a short polite letter back mentioning an October anniversary. Well, my Nan's birthday was in October but also Denise had had her accident in October as well. So I was a little more convinced but still quite disappointed. The next day I went down to a shop in Rochester High Street. The shop was beautiful. They sold crystals, fairy ornaments, beautiful pictures and all things mystical. While I was there, I saw a poster advertising a spiritual church in Chatham. I decided I would like to go there. It said they had clairvoyant evenings on Wednesdays. I felt excited at the thought of going but also very nervous. So I asked three of my friends if they would come with me. On Wednesday, I rang my friends but none of them could come with me. I was really upset because I had asked them because I felt so nervous and didn't want to go by myself. I asked Gary if he would come and he said no as well. Gary said that he wasn't interested in it so I resigned myself to missing the evening. But as time went on I thought to myself, *"Why should I miss out because no-one else would come with me?"* It wasn't the fault of my friends, I understood they were working and one couldn't get a baby-sitter. I realised that if I wanted to go I would have to go by myself. Gary drove me as I wasn't sure where I would park my car. He said he would pick me up when it finished. As I walked in, there were a couple of women at the door who welcomed me and took an entrance fee of £2. I got there quite early and there were only a few people there. I sat about 4 rows from the front, right next to the wall. The church started to get busier. I looked around a few times but I didn't see anyone I knew, so I sat there on my own, feeling more and more nervous. When it started, a man was introduced as the medium. The medium said a prayer and spoke straight to me. I was shaking so much with nerves that I could hardly speak. He said *"you've been seeing shadows."*

"No I haven't" I said.

He said, *"Put it this way, you think you've seen someone but when you look again, they are not there."* I could totally understand that because those were the exact words that I had said to my Mum earlier that day. I thought I'd seen someone standing on the other side of the living room window whilst I was talking to Mum on the phone. I was amazed that the medium had said the exact words. He also told me about my back pain and said I should have healing on it to help. I did have a bad back. I had been working at Tesco's doing shelf filling and my back had been steadily getting worse. He gave me my gran's Christian name which was Lilly, or Lill as she liked to be known. He also gave the name of May but I didn't know who that was. When Gary came to pick me up, I told him all about it. I was so pleased that I had had the courage to go on my own. I got home and rang my Mum. She was really impressed, especially when I told her the medium gave gran's name. Mum also told me that she had an aunty May and that aunty May was my godmother. Mum told me that aunty May and her uncle Frank, had moved out to South Africa the day after I had been christened. Mum had remembered they had both passed away but she couldn't remember when. Well that started the ball rolling. I started going to the spiritualist church more and more, especially on a Sunday when they had a full service. The service was always opened with a prayer and we sang lots of lovely hymns. Then a prayer would be said for the whole world and especially for all the places in the world that needed peace and understanding. The guest medium would give a talk, which was called an address, which I found fascinating. Some mediums would talk about their lives or their experiences. But there were a few who were able to let spirit's speak through them, bringing teachings from the spirit realms. It was at these times, I felt totally at peace and I absolutely loved it. More hymns were sung and then the time came for the medium to give a demonstration of spiritual communication. This part of the service was for the friends and loved ones, who had passed over, to come through and give messages of love and guidance to those who they cared for. I found this wonderful to listen to. It was so wonderful to see people smiling and having tears of joy to hear their family and friends who were still around them. After service, healing was offered to all those who needed it. Soft music was played for the healing and those who wanted to, could go downstairs for a cup of tea and refreshments.

Chapter 14
Healing

I was still working part time for Tesco's, but my back had been getting more and more painful, so one Thursday evening, I told Gary I would like to go to one of the healing sessions at the church. As I drove there, I felt quite nervous because even though I had been to the church a few times by then, I still didn't know anyone there. I wondered if the healing would do me any good. What I didn't know, was that it was going to open up a whole new life for me.

I got to the church and went in, there were just a few people sitting there in seats and there were about six people standing, dressed in white coats. Soft music was playing and I could smell the scent of lavender. The evening sunshine was shining through the windows and where the glass was stained, it was sending the most beautiful colours across the church. I sat down not really knowing what to do and a man in a white coat came up to me and introduced himself as Ron. He had dark grey hair, twinkling eyes and the strongest Scottish accent I had ever heard. As he started talking to me, I felt my nervousness fade away. He told me that when they called me up for healing I was not to worry and just sit down in the chair. After a while an elderly lady called me up to the front. I sat in the chair and Ron also came up. They said a little prayer over me and then, as I sat between them, they put their hands on my head and then slowly all over me, being careful to ask if it was ok to do so. I felt myself closing my eyes and I was aware of wonderful warmth coming from their hands. Although I had my eyes closed, I could see different colours coming towards me. Mostly they were green and purple and they seemed to come over me in waves. I heard Ron say *"Bless you,"* and then he told me to open my eyes. I felt very strange, almost as though I were light-headed and tingly. As I sat there, Ron asked how my back and neck felt and I told him that it felt very warm, as though there was a hot water bottle resting on it. I sat back on the chair near the doors for a while, enjoying the music and watching Ron as he did healing on the others who were waiting.

As I was driving home, the roads seemed extra peaceful and I was aware that somehow I felt different inside. As the evening was so beautiful, I thought I would sit out in the garden. Gary had put the children to bed and was watching television. I got the sun lounger out and laid down on it looking at the sky. There wasn't a cloud to be seen and there was hardly a breeze. The sky was so blue it seemed to wrap itself around me and I could have been anywhere as everything around me just seemed to fade away. Suddenly I had a feeling of déjà vu. I felt myself tingling all over and the feeling was getting stronger. The deep blue of the sky seemed to be moving. I looked and I could see little white specks all moving in the sky. The feeling in me was getting very strong and I started to feel and hear a deep vibration within me. I felt very light, as though I were lifting off of the lounger. Then suddenly I felt a familiar lurch in my stomach and I started to feel very frightened. I jumped up and came indoors. The room seemed so dark after the sun and the blue sky but that feeling in my stomach had been too much and I didn't go back out there that evening. That night when I went to bed I felt so tired. Usually my back would play up in the night but that night I slept straight through. I didn't even remember dreaming, which was very unusual for me. It was the best night's sleep I had had for quite a few years. I continued to go to church to have regular healing on my back. My back and neck were improving a lot. I found, that for some reason, just going to church and having the healing had opened me up to all sorts of wonderful things. Ron and I had become very good friends and in turn friends with my family. He helped me to get over my nervousness and was always on the end of the phone to help me understand things that were starting to happen in my life. I had started to see spirits in my home. They would appear as shadows as I was doing the most mundane chores and I was getting used to seeing wispy smoke as I sat and watched television. I had started to dream of my granddad again, I would talk to him about any worries I had. I would always remember what granddad told me when I woke up and it really helped. My cat, Sparky, had been killed in the road outside our home the year Glen was born and I was seeing him quite regularly. I saw him clearly when I was feeding Missy and I would feel him getting on our bed at night. One morning, I was sitting on the settee having a cup of tea when I saw my gran as clear as day walking down my garden to the back door. This made me very happy as gran had passed away before I had got married so had never physically been to our home.

Ron and I were having coffee one day and my neck was particularly painful. I had caught a draft in it sleeping with the window open. He offered to give me some healing and I sat for about ten minutes as he did healing on my neck and shoulders. When he had finished, he stood up and leaned against the wall, we were talking and suddenly I noticed a blue outline around his body. As we spoke the blue outline grew to about 6 inches all around him. Ron noticed that I wasn't really paying attention to what he was saying and asked if I was ok. I told him what I could see around him and he laughed and said, *"I don't believe it, you're seeing auras already and you've only been doing this for a short time."* (Of course I had forgotten all about what I had been able to see in my childhood). Ron told me that the reason his aura was blue, was because he had been giving me healing. He said that to see aura's all, I had to do was to relax my eyes and look a few inches above the person or object. As he told me this, it seemed somehow that I already knew what he meant which really puzzled me. I said to him that I thought it was the energy I was seeing. He said that was right and we spent the rest of the day trying to see auras on all sorts of things. When I got home I told Mum how to do it and I rang my Dad and told him as well. I wanted to share this with everyone that I knew so they would be able to see them as well. When I rang Colin, he said that he had always seen auras. Well that took the wind out of my sails. I was astonished. I asked him why he had never said anything about it before. He said that he never thought that it was unusual and he assumed that everybody saw them. I also found out that he also saw spirits and heard them too. It seemed that it wasn't unusual for our family even my Gran had seen spirit at times. As I learnt more and more I realised that everybody was capable of seeing, sensing and hearing spirits. All of Gary's family had also seen spirits at one time or another.

Chapter 15
Small steps

At my church, they were holding meditation groups and beginners circles. Ron said that it would be a good idea for me to join the meditation group. He knew of my frightening experiences by then and he said that meditation would help me understand more and help me to take the fear away. This sounded great, so one evening I went down to the meditation group. There were about ten people there and they were seated on chairs in the church, in a big circle. The circle was run by a woman called Nikki. I had met her briefly in church and she was very friendly and full of laughter, that put everybody at ease. She opened up the evening in prayer and then put some gentle music on. She told us to close our eyes and relax and we had to listen to her telling a story and imagine what she was saying. Nikki told us that our spirit guides would draw close to us and we might see or hear things in our mind that went with the meditation she was telling us. I closed my eyes and she started talking about going on a walk in the countryside. She said there was a waterfall and we were to stand beneath, it feeling the spray on our faces. After a while she said our guides would come and talk to us and we should remember what they said. I tried to imagine what she was saying but it was really difficult for me. I could see clouds of purple and violet moving around, then I had a strange feeling come all around me. It felt like a cushion of soft warm air. It got stronger and then I felt frightened and I could feel the pounding of my heart, so I opened my eyes and waited until everyone else had opened theirs. They all looked very relaxed as they sat there in deep meditation and it seemed to take forever before the others had finished. When they had all finished, Nikki went around everyone in turn to find out what they were given. They were talking about the most wonderful things they had seen, animals, loved ones, angels and guides. They were all giving the most fantastic stories and I'm ashamed to say it, but I thought they were all making it up. When Nikki came to me she said that she knew I had felt frightened. She said I had a guide who was a man of the desert, a nomad, and he would help me overcome my fear. Once that had happened there would be lots for me. Well I really wanted to believe her but I didn't have any proof that what she said was correct. Although she was right when she said about the fear I felt, so perhaps there was something in it after all. When the evening had finished, I sat out in the car park with Ron, talking over my experience. He told me not to worry and even went as far as saying that one day I'll be doing healing and giving messages just like the mediums did. Well, when he said this I just laughed in his face. As far as I was concerned he was just talking a load of nonsense to make me feel better, and if I ever had to speak out loud to a stranger I was usually shaking like a jelly. I went to the meditation group on a regular basis and it was really good for me because I gradually got to know all the people there quite well. I relaxed more and more but when it came to the meditation I still wasn't getting anything, but even so I found it fascinating to hear the stories of everyone else. Very gradually, I realised that what they were getting in their meditations were not made up, because of the emotions that some of them had brought back. One evening, as we went into meditation, I felt a warm tingly feeling upon my face; it didn't scare me because it felt so gentle. In my meditation I saw myself as a little girl and I was holding a man's hand. I didn't know the man but I felt safe with him. He was very tall and a lot older than I was. We were standing in the darkness on the edge of a kerbstone, waiting to cross the road. The vision ended and I started getting the purple and violet waves of light coming over me. When the meditation finished, Nikki came to me and I told her exactly what I had seen. She said that my barrier that I had put there to stop me being frightened, was starting to come down. My spirit guides were taking things very slowly with me and it was starting to pay off because I was relaxing more and more in meditation. Nikki told me that with some people it was the complete opposite. They want the contact so much that they concentrate too much on getting visions and it causes a blockage. Well, I was over the moon. It seemed so little compared to what the others in the group had got but it meant so much to me. So the next morning, I thought that I would try to do a little meditation myself. It was a very warm day although the sky was overcast. So I decided to sit out in the garden to try meditating. As I sat there the air seemed extra still and it was so quiet, even the birds had stopped singing. There was no noise at all, other than the creak of my chair when I moved. It was as though the whole world had gone silent for my meditation. I closed my eyes and said a prayer, asking my guides and loved ones to draw close to me and asking God for protection. I deepened my breathing and I could feel myself getting heavier as I relaxed more and more. Then colours came, wonderful colours that I had never seen before, moving towards me slowly as I relaxed deeper and deeper. Then the colours started to move faster and faster. It was like I was going through a tunnel. They were going really fast and I suddenly felt myself get very light and it frightened the wits out of me. My eyes shot open and my heart was thumping. I could feel tears in my eyes and then I felt somebody stroke my cheek to calm me down. As I sat there staring in front of me, I felt my heart slowing down and I could feel myself relaxing again. I was aware of a wonderful feeling of love coming from whoever was with me. It was a long time though before I tried it again on my own.

The next day, I was playing with Glen and I saw a man walk across my living room. He was about my age and wore a black suit with a dazzling white shirt. He had short, wavy, dark brown hair and he was so handsome but I had no idea who he was. Two weeks later I saw him again, this time it was when I was at Ron's house. I was really puzzled and I mentioned it to Ron. He didn't really have any answers either. Later on that day, I spoke to Mum and told her what I'd seen. Mum said that she had also seen him when she was staying at our house one weekend, but she didn't like to say anything to me in case it frightened me. Mum had no idea either who he was but the thing that we both realised was that he was connected to me in some way. A few months afterwards, I was sitting in the church and the medium came to me with a message. She said to me that there had been a miscarriage in the family. I disagreed because I hadn't heard of anyone losing a baby in our family. But still the medium insisted, and she also said that the miscarriage was a boy and she said that babies continue to grow in the spirit realms, so even though she had been shown a baby she said that he was a fully grown man now. The medium said that the baby had been called David. Well, as usual, with anything I was given at church I would ring Mum up afterwards to tell her all about it. When I mentioned the miscarriage Mum said that she had a miscarriage a very long time ago when I was a young child. Then she told me that she loved the name David so it was quite possible that she would have given him that name. Suddenly the penny dropped: Mum said that she thought the spirit that we had both seen recently was David, and then Mum said that she thought that my invisible friend was called

David. I had forgotten all about him as I had grown older. But what Mum said had just felt so right and made perfect sense. I knew then that I had a brother on the Earth plain who was Colin, and a brother in the spirit realms called David. Also David was looking after me as he had done so many years ago. I saw David a couple more times after that. But only for a few seconds, I haven't seen him since. I feel he was just coming back to let me know he was still around and who he really was. I can imagine him talking with my sister now and it makes me feel so happy to know that I have ultimate proof that life is eternal.

One evening I was putting Glen to bed and he asked, *"Why does my bed keep on bouncing?"* I asked him what he meant and he said that he could feel the end of his bed going up and down when he was laying in it. I knew immediately that he could feel spirits sitting on the end of his bed. That was exactly what it had felt like to me. Well I didn't want to say that it was his imagination because I had remembered that when I was told that it made me more frightened. So I told him that it was Jesus watching over him and he did this with all the babies and children in the world. This didn't frighten him as he prayed to Jesus and God in school. That evening, after I had put him to bed I came downstairs and told Gary. Richard heard what I was saying and he told me that he had also felt that. As Richard was three years older than Glen I told him a little more. I said that it could be Jesus or it could be his aunty Denise, or in fact anyone who had gone to heaven and was watching over us. Richard said he knew that people didn't die because he had seen our cat Sparky quite a few times since he had been killed. I was amazed because he had never said anything and thankfully didn't seem to be frightened either. Everybody in my family could see spirit and that really helped me because my children weren't frightened.

When I was at church next, I told Nikki about my children. She told me that all babies and young children see spirit and auras. Most can communicate with spirit as well. This is quite often why babies seem to look past you and start smiling and cooing, because they can see what we can't. I found out that a lot of children lose this ability to see and communicate with the spirit world as they grow older. This is so they can concentrate on school and life, but some children keep their spiritual gifts all of their lives and it can sometimes make growing up very difficult. Most of the people who belonged to the church seemed to have had strong spiritual experiences when they were children and I saw that how coming to places like a spiritual church or centre, really helped them understand these things. I also saw how people were comforted with the knowledge and proof that their loved ones were still around them. I was very much drawn to the healing side of the church as I saw a great improvement not only in myself but also in others who had healing on a regular basis.

Chapter 16
A wonderful energy

Ron asked me one day if I would like to try giving him healing. He told me to sit in front of him and relax and then holding my hand in front of him with my palm open, move my hands slowly over him without touching. He told me to stop wherever I felt a change of some sort. I did this and when my hand moved over his chest on the top left hand side I felt my hand go very hot. All of a sudden I saw a bright electric blue flash on his other shoulder. It was about the size of a saucer. I carried on moving my hands down and the same thing happened when I got to his knees. I continued down to his feet and both of my hands were absolutely buzzing with energy. Where I had felt my hands go hot on his chest and shoulder, Ron told me that he had had an accident years before that had left his chest and shoulder out of line and extremely painful. He also said that the accident had left both his knees damaged and he had metal plates in both of his knees. He asked me if I would rest my hands on these places and ask my healing guide to draw close and give Ron healing. I didn't even know I had a healing guide. Anyway, I asked my guide to draw close and, as I did, I felt a warm feeling all over my body. I lay my hands on Ron's chest and shoulder, and then his knees and my hands got hotter and hotter. After about ten minutes Ron said that the pain had gone and all he could feel was warmth. This was the first time I had ever done healing and it felt wonderful while I was doing it. Ron explained that everybody that does healing is a channel for God's energy. The energy travels through you while you are giving healing. I also found that this wonderful energy coming through me to Ron, was helping my aches and pains as well. Ron told me that he thought I should take a healing course and that way I could learn more about it, and I would have a certificate to say I could do healing on anyone, if they wished me to. This sounded like a wonderful idea, so I approached the head healer at the church and after a couple of weeks I started my training as a healer. I made arrangements for my friend to pick my children up from school on a Monday, and every Monday I went to the church to learn and train in healing. Whilst I was training, I found that I was becoming more sensitive. I would be near people and feel their pain: if they had a headache, I would have one. If they had a toothache, I would have it as well. The pains would go as soon as I asked them about the pains.

One day when I was training, a woman of about thirty came in for healing. She was very worried because she had been diagnosed with a brain tumour. She came to healing every Monday and most of the time she would bring her daughter with her who was about three years old. Her daughter had long brown hair and beautiful big brown eyes. She would sit quietly with crayons whilst her Mum was having healing. She was so good, a perfect little angel. Her Mum told us that the healing always helped her relax and since she started coming the tumour had stopped growing. We couldn't say of course that the healing had done this but as long as it was relaxing her anything else was a wonderful bonus. One day my trainer and I were giving a gentleman healing, when I saw them walk through the doors of the church and there was a pretty little girl with blond curly hair holding her daughter's hand. The girl was about the same age and they were both smiling. After we had finished giving the gentleman healing, I looked up and asked the woman to come over and sit for her healing. Her little girl sat quietly as usual doing her colouring but the other little girl was nowhere to be seen. I asked her Mum where she was. Her Mum didn't know who I meant. I said *"The little girl who came in with your daughter, they were holding hands."*

"There wasn't anyone with us," she said. It was then I realised that I had seen a spirit. I told her that her daughter must have an invisible friend and I was amazed that I had seen her so clearly, as to think she was real. But then again she was real just like my invisible friend had been to me

It took me two years to complete my training and I was given my certificate so I could offer healing to my friends and do healing without supervision. Then an absent healing group had been started at my church. There was only about five of us in the group but it was lovely. A candle was lit and we took it in turns to open up in prayer and then we would say the Lord's Prayer together. After that we would give out all the names of people that we knew who needed God's healing. Then the leader of our group would take us on a meditation and she told us this meditation was for us, so we could enjoy the healing that the angels gave us. After this we would close in prayer and go home. The evening was quite short but it was such a lovely time for us. Even though I had done healing for a while now, I was still full of questions. I wanted to know why a candle was always lit. I felt really stupid asking but no-one had ever told me why this was done. I was told that the lighting of a candle enforces the power of the prayer. As it was a healing group, it helped with the healing in the room. The flame represents the light of God and all that is holy. So this also helps to dispel any negative energy. The fact that we said the Lord's Prayer with a lit candle also made everything more powerful. I was also told that when the flame was blown out at the end of the evening, you should dedicate the flame to something good, world peace for example. I realised that there was nothing stupid about asking this because now the lighting of a candle not only made sense but I found it very beautiful. My meditations were becoming more visual now. I would see many different things and the other people's stories didn't seem so strange. In the healing group, we always had a meditation and quite often we would go to a huge tree on a big hill, this was known as our healing tree. We would sometimes see the others in our group by this tree, quite often we appeared in each other's meditation, it would always amaze me and I always had lovely experiences. One particular evening we were in a meditation where we walked across a stream and I could actually feel the coolness of the stream on my feet and legs. I could feel the warmth of the sun on my face and I was shown a beautiful rainbow. It was so relaxing. Then all of a sudden, to my horror, I saw the face of the demon girl in the exorcist film that had frightened me so much. It wasn't there for long, probably only a second or two but it was there all the same. I came out of my meditation that instant and I felt really scared. The leader of the group could see that I was upset and told me to drink some water. She asked me what happened and I told her, she said that why it was in my meditation was because it had caused me emotional problems and sooner or later I had to face my fear. She said it had happened there because I was in the best place for it to happen, in a healing sanctuary with candles and friends. Spirit weren't trying to frighten the life out of me they were trying to help me get over my fear. This was one of the last hurdles that I had to get over. Well, the next time I went to the healing group, I must admit that I felt really worried in case I saw the face again, but thankfully I never did.

A week later, I had the most beautiful experience in the middle of the night. I woke up to find myself lying on my stomach which was most unusual. As I lifted my head up to turn over, I saw the most beautiful sparkling star on the wall above me. It was about eighteen inches in size and it was more brilliant than the brightest white you could imagine. It reminded me of the sparkler fireworks that you get. It was the shape of the star of Bethlehem and it was the most beautiful thing I had ever seen. I would love to be shown it again. I know that God showing me this meant that I was, and still am, truly blessed. A good friend of mine told me that the star is a sign of divine love and the brilliant white is the purity of divine love and both mean that God is with me. Well I have no doubt that God is with me, in more ways than one. I could not live this life without that knowledge. God brings me light in a darkened world. God brings me peace, love and understanding. God provides me with everything I need and almost everything I have asked for. I know that I only have to be patient and whatever I need is provided.

Chapter 17
If I can do it, you can too

I was coming on very well in both of my groups seeing, hearing and sensing spirit more and more. I decided it was time to join a development group. This would help me understand the gifts that God was giving me and I would learn to use them. This made me a little sad because I had to give up my meditation group, which I thoroughly enjoyed. This was because I would have been out too many nights on the trot. It wasn't going down well with Gary that I was going out more in the evenings. I did invite him to join me, especially on a Sunday when we could all go, but alas he wasn't interested. This made me feel very sad because amazing things were happening in my life and I couldn't share it with him. As he told me, he just wasn't interested. As luck would have it the development circle had always had a meditation in it, so that was great, I wasn't going to miss it after all. In the circle, I learnt how to sense when spirit were near me and sometimes I would see a gold shimmering light next to me. I learnt that by holding someone's hands when I was trying to get messages for them, it would help them to relax and strengthen the link. I also learnt that drinking water was very important. If a spirit was a little emotional, drinking water would help keep me calm and if I had trouble finishing a link with someone, drinking water would help with that too. Water is also a wonderful carrier of spiritual energy. Sometimes we would see spirit faces in the water and if we asked for a blessing from God on the water, it had a much nicer taste as well.

One evening when I was at home, I was lying on the sofa feeling very weary. It seemed far too early to go to bed and there wasn't much on television that I was interested in, so I drifted off to sleep. I was dreaming that I was at the church, standing near the front, when I noticed a man in desert dress standing in front of me. He didn't smile, but just looked at me. Then I felt a strong, tingly feeling all over me and I felt afraid, somehow I woke myself up and as I opened my eyes I had a feeling of floating down into my body. I lay there for a minute or two feeling a little dizzy. Then I got up and got a drink of water. The dizziness went and as I sat there, I realised what had happened. Somehow I had floated out of my body, and even though there was noise from the television it hadn't stopped me or disturbed me. The feeling of floating down had been really nice, it was seeing the man that had startled me. Then I remembered that quite a while ago, it may have even been a year before, Nikki had told me that I had a man from the desert as my guide. This really excited me as I has tried to see my guide in meditation many times but had been unsuccessful. Now, when I least expected it, I had seen him. I did wonder why he wasn't smiling but nevertheless I was ecstatic. My tiredness had completely gone and at 1 AM, I was awake and still full of smiles. When I got to group the following week, I told Nikki and she was so pleased for me. She told me that he was my life guide and this meant that he had been with me when I was born and he would stay with me guiding me until it was my time to go back to the spirit world. I asked if he was with me when I was giving healing. She said that he always stood in the background when I did healing and another guide stepped forward to work through me. She told me that I had a sister of mercy as a healing guide and she wouldn't be surprised if I saw her as well. I later found out that we have all sorts of spirits that help us on our journey of life. We have our loved ones who have passed over and often come around to help us or guide us. Then we have our life guides that are with us for the whole of our Earth life, and guides who take us through different stages of our development. We also have spirit helpers that are there to help us with situations in our lives. For example, if we need courage to make a change in our life, we may get a helper who is very strong. This can even be an animal helper like a lion or if we need to be a bit tougher we may get a rhino. We may have had a relation who was very strong willed and if this person has passed over they may come back to give their strong energy to us. Then there are beings from other dimensions that can also guide us. These beings are usually very advanced in spiritual matters and some of them come to pass on their wonderful knowledge to us. There are also many ascended masters who help and teach us. Ascended masters are spirits that have lived on the Earth plane in a physical body and they are filled with such compassion for all mankind and all living things that they shine with God's love and light. They help to teach us many things and often work with the angels and archangels to help bring peace, healing, love and understanding to everyone on our planet. The angels and archangels can also come as guides and helpers. If only everyone knew that there was so much help available to us and all we have to do is ask God for the help we need. As the well-known Star Trek phrase goes "Its life Jim, but not as we know it."

My church had a psychic fair running on a Saturday morning and I decided to go along to it. There were several mediums sitting at tables, giving readings, and all sorts of refreshments. There were people selling crystals and relaxation music on cds. There were lots of pretty gifts to buy and the place was buzzing with energy. I decided that I would like a reading, so I booked with a woman who had the most beautiful blonde curly hair. She looked very friendly and I was drawn to her immediately. She told me that I had been very lonely in my life and that there was a woman that I knew who I was going to become great friends with. She also said that people told me their deepest secrets and often they would burst into tears in my company. This was very true because I found more and more friends would divulge their innermost fears and secrets and say that they had never told anyone else this before. Then they would cry, releasing the tension that had built up for years. The medium told me that that was what I was here for, to make people feel better. But she told me that I was taking on other people's emotions while I was helping them and I had to let the emotions go. I wasn't sure whether I believed this but I kept an open mind, although I have to say, that even as she spoke I felt myself near to tears. She said that the best way to release these emotions was to put on a sad film and have a good cry, this would help all the emotions come out. Well I got the bus home after the fair and it was all I could do to stop bawling my head off on the bus. I decided that I would take her advice and have a good grizzle when I got home, to get it out of my system. Well, when I arrived home my Dad was there. He had come down for a surprise visit. That really mucked up my plans No way was I going to cry in front of anyone else, even if it was my Dad, so I pushed my emotions back down where I could control them and carried on regardless. On the Monday it happened, I was washing up and I was all alone in the house and the tears came. It was always when I was alone that the crying continued. For three weeks I grizzled on and off and then it stopped. It was a big lesson not to take on other people's problems. I now knew the effect that it would have on me if I did. What the medium said about a new friend coming into my life also came very true. It was at Glen's infant school I started talking

84

to a woman called Ann. I had seen her at school for quite a while but she seemed to be close friends with others there, so we only ever acknowledged one another by saying hello and goodbye. One morning, I had been talking to someone in the playground about the church I was going to. I didn't tend to say much about it outside: I suppose that I thought that people wouldn't be interested. I was also aware of how people tended to keep away from those who attended church because of fear of being brain washed. However, as I walked outside the school and crossed the road, Ann came up to me. She said that she had overheard me talking and had often wanted to go to a spiritual church but she didn't know anyone who she could go with. Ann came with me and grew to love the church as I did. She and I became good friends, looking after each other's children when we needed help. Ann had also had spiritual experiences and started to develop in the groups at church as well.

One morning Ann came round for a coffee and chat, and we decided to give each other readings. This went really well and I gave Ann lots of information about her childhood and about her parents. When it was Ann's turn she told me she could feel her head hurting badly on one side. Then she said she was being shown a car crash, but she was being shown it as though she were above the accident. Ann said then that the picture had gone and she could see very dark grey around her. She felt that she could hear people talking around a bed but she couldn't feel anything. I realised that she had got Denise with her and Denise was describing the accident that she was in. Ann said that Denise had felt frightened when the grey was around her and she felt sick. Then the grey started to fade into purple and get lighter and lighter. Denise felt herself floating upwards away from the darkness, and she saw my gran and pop waiting for her and then it felt like she went to sleep. I knew that the time that Denise was surrounded in grey was when she was on the life support machine in the hospital. When the machine was switched off she was allowed to continue her journey back home to the spirit realms. We never realised that Denise was aware of us in the hospital until that message. Even though the message made us a little sad, it was wonderful to know the truth of what Denise had told us. Ann was over the moon that her first reading meant so much and she went on to grow into a wonderful medium.

I was sitting in meditation one day and I was told that I should do more healing, so when I was visiting Mum I told her what spirit had said. Mum said *"Well you give me healing on my back, how about doing healing on my foot?"* Mum had got a bunion on her left foot and when she showed it to me, it was very red and inflamed. She hadn't been to the doctor's because the operation to have them removed was also very painful and that worried her. I gave Mum healing on her foot for the next 3 weeks and the following month she showed me her foot. The bunion had completely gone. I couldn't believe it, there was no lump, and no redness, absolutely nothing to show it had ever been there, amazing. After that I decided to invite my friends to my home to offer healing if they needed it. A couple of people said I should charge for healing but I didn't because I always had healing for free so why should I charge others. My friends started to come around my home for healing on Wednesday mornings. My friends always said they felt better afterwards and some would see colours in the room as I gave healing. We had another cat by then and we had named him Pumpkin. Every time I started my healing, Pumpkin would appear from nowhere and he would sit underneath the chair that people would have healing on and as soon as I had finished the healing session, Pumpkin would disappear back to wherever he had come from. This happened every time without fail. He was a very special cat to me, there was just something different about him. If ever any of us were ill he would always jump up on our laps and lay as close as he could to us, even if it meant that he was right up on our chest. I have read that it has now been scientifically proved that the purring that a cat gives resonates with our bodies and promotes direct healing. So maybe Pumpkin knew that he was helping us feel better. I thought about this many times and then Pumpkin made me realise that he absolutely knew what I needed. It was in the October about twelve years ago. I was going through a particularly emotional time and normally things wouldn't get me down for very long. If I felt fed up or depressed, I would give myself a good talking to and put a comedy on. Then I would snap out of it in no time at all. But that day I just felt that I wanted to cry all the time. I was all on my own, the children were at school, Gary was at work and I was so unhappy. I opened the kitchen door and walked out into my garden. The day was very dark and mild, and it looked like the heavens were going to open anytime. I sat on the step in my garden just staring into oblivion. I could feel the odd tear gently sliding down my cheek. I sat there feeling thoroughly miserable when I felt Pumpkin sit on the step next to me. Then he got up on his back two legs and put one of his paws on my shoulder as if to show me he cared and he was there for me. This made me cry even more as a feeling of love swept over me. As I looked towards my back door I saw a cloud of emerald green colour spreading like a soft mist up the path and then it was all over me. I sobbed and sobbed realising that no matter how lonely I felt, I always had God and Pumpkin.

Chapter 18
My daughter

I was given a message one night when I was at a clairvoyant evening at church. The medium told me that there was a baby coming to the Earth plane and gave me the month of September for the birth. The message didn't mean anything to me at the time and I certainly didn't think spirit meant me as I had the coil fitted after I had Glen. But early January I found out that I had fallen pregnant. Even though it wasn't planned, Gary and I were very pleased about the news and we started to make plans. By February we had told a few people, but not everyone knew. My friends at church knew because they had heard the message that the medium had given me previously and I had told them it was me. On the 16th February, in the afternoon, I started to get dreadful stomach cramps and started to bleed. Gary came home early and we rang the doctor who told us to go straight up to the hospital. By around 8oclock that evening I knew that I had miscarried. We were both extremely upset and it was very late by the time we got to bed. The following day, I was taken back up the hospital and stayed in overnight to have a D&C which was to clean everything away that had been left behind. The doctor said that even though it was very sad I should never have fallen pregnant in the first place as I had been fitted with the coil. I was lying in the hospital bed and all was quiet. It was about 11.30 at night and I was to be one of the last patients to go down to theatre. Everyone else seemed to be asleep and I thought, well if this doesn't shake my faith in spirit, nothing will. Spirit had said there was a baby coming to the Earth, I fell pregnant. They gave September as a birth month and, had the baby gone full term, it would have been born in September. Yes I felt upset but I was also amazed that the message had been correct. Just then I saw a huge blue flash of light on the opposite wall of the ward and then I felt my Mum hold my hand. Even though Mum was frightened of astral travel, if she thought that Colin or I were in trouble and she couldn't physically be with us, she could just shut her eyes and think herself with us and she would travel to our location. Mum had done this with my brother when he was travelling back from her late one night. It was after New Year's Day and the roads were thick with snow. As Colin left, Mum made Colin promise to ring her when he got home. Colin had moved down to Strood and it took an hour on a good night to get home. Mum was so worried because of the treacherous roads that she astral travelled above his car all the way until he got to his front door. When Colin rang her to say he was home safely Mum was able to prove she was with him by telling him the cars that were in front of him and behind him as he drove home.

The day after my operation, I was allowed home and Mum and Dad came down to see me. Mum told me that she had had a vision of our baby and she was a little girl. She had seen her being held by my gran and she was in a christening gown. That made me feel so much better and even though some people might say Mum was just saying that to make me feel better, I was soon to have more proof from spirit that our baby was ok. I had a few phone calls from my friends, and one of them from my church said to me that losing the baby was a lesson for me. I was very upset by this and wondered how she could say such a thing to me. It seemed a cruel and heartless thing to say. I now know that what she meant, that it was part of my life experience to go through, and I understand now that we have to go through many things in our lives for one reason or another. But at the time it was the last thing I needed to hear. The soul that chooses to come to the Earth plane may come just to experience what it is to be conceived, to be in a mother's womb. The soul may be born and continue into childhood or adulthood, depending on what the soul is here to learn or experience. Where there is an abortion or still born birth to experience, the soul of that baby makes a spiritual contract with the spirit of the mother and father, and it is agreed how to help the baby end its life. So as sad as it made me, I know that my baby girl chose to physically be with me for just a few weeks. About three weeks later, I returned to church and the guest medium that night was an elderly man by the name of Fred; I took to him straight away as he reminded me of my granddad Hyne. The service was lovely and afterwards we all went downstairs for a cup of tea. I sat next to Fred and as we were chatting, he suddenly asked me if I knew someone that had just lost a baby. I said yes, but I didn't elaborate. He then said he was shown a vision of a baby girl in a long white gown and he had to tell me that she had been baptised. I smiled and told Fred that the baby belonged to me and it was confirmation of what Mum had said to me. I was so happy and of course rang Mum straight away; she was thrilled to bits as well. I also told Gary. He half smiled, the problem was that unfortunately Gary didn't tend to believe a lot of what I said to him, which was a shame because it meant that I kept a lot to myself, but I realise now that everybody needs their own proof. A couple of months later, I stayed over my Mums with Richard and Glen. The boys slept downstairs on a sofa bed and I slept upstairs in the back bedroom. In the middle of the night, I was woken up by a movement next to me and the sound of a baby cooing. I opened my eyes and I saw my baby girl lying next to me on my bed. I played with her and cuddled her and then the next thing, I opened my eyes and it was morning. I knew it wasn't a dream because it was real and I knew that I had been out of my body playing with my baby girl. I'm so lucky that I constantly see her. She's growing up and now I see her as a young teenager with beautiful long brown hair. I often wondered what her name was as we didn't really choose a name. So I decided that I would name her Rosie. One morning as I woke up I heard her voice clearly saying, "Mum, I love my name."

Chapter 19
Who am I?

I seemed to be developing more and more, especially at night time, which seemed strange as I had been so afraid of the dark for most of my life. But maybe that was God's way of making me realise that there was nothing to be afraid of. Nearly every night, after I said my prayers, I would see visions. Many things would be shown to me. All parts of our Earth, places I would never be likely to visit, stars and planets, people I didn't know and family and friends that had passed over, animals etc. I also saw colours that were so beautiful because the colours seemed alive. Sometimes I would see black, not frightening black but wonderful deep velvet black that would envelope me and with it would come a feeling of extreme peace. My dreams were becoming more vivid as well. I had always dreamt a lot and still do, but now if I don't have at least three different dreams a night, it's very unusual. It wasn't long after I had seen my baby girl at Mums, that I had one of the strangest dreams ever. I dreamt I was at church, in our beginners circle. Nikki was teaching as usual, then all of a sudden I started speaking in the group. Nikki stopped talking and everyone in the circle turned to listen to what I was saying. My voice was really deep and gravelly and I sounded like a male. My body was dark red and scaly and I had long fingers with long claws, I was aware that my head had changed shape and I had no hair. In the chairs where the congregation would sit on a Sunday, were all manner of religious people who were listening intently to what I was saying. There were nuns and bishops, popes, priests and ministers, so many people and they were dressed in beautiful colours rather than the dark colours that we are used to seeing them wear. They seemed to be in colours of lemon, lavender and a beautiful light blue. I could hear myself talking but I can't remember what I was talking about. I felt myself going slightly dizzy in my dream and then a familiar tingling came all over my body. I remember feeling a little frightened and then I woke up. I looked at the clock; it was 4 in the morning. I seemed to be waking up at this time on a regular basis so I wasn't surprised at the time. I went back to sleep until the alarm went off at 7. I couldn't stop thinking about what had happened. I didn't feel worried about it; I just wanted to know what it meant. I didn't tell anyone about it because I didn't want people to say I was crackers. After all, how do you bring into the conversation I dreamt I was an alien last night. No I defiantly thought it was best to keep it to myself. Two weeks later I was in the group at church and Nikki took us into meditation. It was a healing meditation where we were sending healing to our Earth. While I was in meditation I was shown my hands on my lap and they had changed. To my amazement they had become the hands of the red skimmed alien that I had dreamt off. I could see the elongated fingers and the claws. I came out of my meditation and I was very pleased that my hands looked normal again. This time I told Nikki and the group about my hands and I just said that I had seen the same hands in a dream before. I didn't go into details because I still felt worried about what everyone would think. Nikki said that there are spiritual beings who visit us from other dimensions and some come to guide us. So maybe a new guide was showing himself to me. Well that satisfied me a little more but I couldn't help thinking that there was more to it than that.

I had enjoyed my time at church and had made many good friends. Some of the mediums who came regularly remembered me and I got on well with everybody. I was asked if I would like to go onto the church committee and I was so proud to do this. I enjoyed welcoming people into the church and helping them with any questions that I could. I realised that the more I learnt about the spirit world and their ways the less afraid I was. I knew now that the feelings that frightened me as a child were just spirit's energy touching my energy. I wanted to let people know that there was so much more to life than just getting up, working and going to bed. I also wanted people to know God's love. It is in everything and everybody, no matter whom or what they are, or do. The knowledge that was helping me would help others as well. One of the things I loved about all that I was learning was that the more I knew, the more there was to know. Answers brought more questions and my thirst for knowledge opened many wonderful doors. It was the total opposite of how I was at school. I was never very academic, maths was my worst subject and the other subjects weren't far behind. The only ones I was any good at were art and human biology.

Chapter 20
Protection

One of the things I learnt about, was the importance of spiritual protection. When I was first told about this, it conjured up all sorts of frightening images, but then I learnt about why it was necessary and what it would do for me. Because I was becoming more sensitive to the energy of spirit, I was also becoming more sensitive to other energy around me. If people were in bad moods, I would pick up on their moods and feel grouchy. If people were close to me and they needed healing, my energy would constantly go to them leaving me feeling very tired. I would walk into a room and even if there had been an argument while I wasn't there the energy from what had gone on would affect me. Emotionally I was all over the place. A healer in the church told me about the simple process of putting a bubble of protection around myself and it would prevent all of these things affecting me. It seemed such a simple thing to do, so how could it work. All I had to do was imagine a bubble, like a bubble that children blow and imagine myself in this bubble. I was to do this in the morning before I went out of the house. I found the easiest thing to do was to think of it as an extra item of clothing as I got dressed, and that way I rarely forgot to do it. But if I did forget, as soon as I remembered I would put it around me, no matter how late in the day it was. After all, a little protection is better than none at all. What a difference it made, I was astonished. My energy levels rose and headaches went and I was back to being happy me. Also I found out that the more we develop spiritually, the brighter our internal light shines. Our light will attract all sorts of people to us. Some will come for healing, whether it's guidance, laughter or hands-on healing. Spirits will come as well, some to teach and guide, and some who are, what you may call, negative or bad spirits. To be honest I don't believe there are bad spirits, just spirits who should know better, much like us. The animals are also sensitive to our internal light, so many are drawn to us, physical animals or spirit animals. They come because of the unconditional love that is coming from our inner light. Even though I had had my proof that my protection was working, it's very easy to become complacent about it, so spirit taught me the importance of it. I didn't understand why at the time but now I teach others to develop; I understand that protection is paramount.

It happened one Sunday evening when I was at church. There was a man who looked like he was in his mid-thirties. He had started coming in to church for a cup of tea after the service. I don't ever remember him coming for the whole service. On the odd occasion, he would ask for healing and we gave him healing. I don't know what it was about him but my gut feeling told me to be on my guard. So when he wanted healing, I would always make sure that I had another healer with me, preferably a male. That Sunday he turned up when the service was finished and demanded a cup of tea. Normally we would give anyone a free cup but this time I was told that he would have to pay for tea as our funds were short, so any money taken would be appreciated. He was told to pay and he put a few pennies on the plate. I happened to notice that one of the pennies had chocolate stuck to it, but other than that there was nothing unusual. When most of the people had gone it was my job to count up the tea money. I took the money and started to count it, when a terrible feeling came over me. I froze and I felt so sick, the feeling spread over me like treacle. I had tears in my eyes and a dreadful feeling in my stomach. My friend, who was waiting with me, looked at my face and asked me what the matter was. I just couldn't speak and I started shaking all over. It was a good few minutes before I could say anything. I opened my hand and the coin in my hand was the one that had chocolate on it. I didn't know what that man had done but I knew it was something terrible. Had he murdered or raped someone? I didn't know, and I didn't want to know but I knew I had picked up the terrible energy of what he had done. When I was thinking about this later on, I wondered if I had forgotten to put up my bubble of protection. I wasn't sure, but one thing I knew was, that I would never forget again, and the strange thing was that man never came back to the church again.

I started asking for protection for all of my family and pets, every day and every night when I was saying my prayers and I would find myself saying the Lord's Prayer if I felt worried at night. I had been having quite a few dreams when I could feel myself floating and sometimes I would see people I didn't know, appearing in my bedroom. One night as I was laying in my bed, I heard loud noises in my bedroom, like loud cracks and pops. I would get strange noises in my head like loud buzzing and vibrations. The vibrations would get louder and louder and start spreading over my body. I would become very frightened and that would bring nightmares on. They would usually be about the house that I grew up in; I suppose that was because I was really frightened there when I was small. I would then wake up and my heart would be thumping away, I would go down and get a drink then go back to sleep. Sometimes when these noises happened, I would start to feel a lifting sensation but the noises and vibrations were too much and I would wake up terrified. I found this would happen more if I went to bed extremely tired. I knew I was trying to come out of my body and I could just about accept that but it was the noise that scared me. What was worse for me, was that nobody seemed to know what the noises were. I asked everybody I could think of, even the teachers at church but nobody had any answers for me. One afternoon I was meditating and my guide drew very close to me. I asked my guide what the noises were. He said that like the noise of the waves on the ocean, you cannot have one without the other. I understood that the vibration was all part of me leaving my body. I was just going to have to get used to it, but that was easier said than done. Over and over again I experienced the noises and every time it happened I woke myself up to stop it. After a few months, things calmed down and the vibrations and the noises stopped.

Glen was now seven years old and Richard was now ten. I had decided that I would like another baby. Gary and I hadn't realised how much we wanted another child until I had miscarried. I fell pregnant and our baby was due in November. We didn't tell many people in the beginning because of what had happened before but by the time I was 5 months everyone knew and was pleased for us. In the October, I was at church and the medium called Fred was there, the one who reminded me of granddad. When he was giving messages he asked if anyone was having out of body experiences. I put up my hand and he said "spirit is saying that you're very frightened of it." I agreed and he told me just to relax and go with it and I would have some wonderful experiences. Two weeks later, I was asleep in bed and started to feel the vibrations and hear the noises. They got stronger and stronger and I started to feel frightened. Then I saw Fred's face in my mind and I remembered his words. Somehow I managed to relax and the noises and vibrations faded away, then I was moving diagonally up and out of my bedroom window. I could see purple clouds moving fast beneath me and I could feel the air buffeting under me. I seemed to be flying faster and faster and then, suddenly, I was standing on a top landing in the dark. I thought that I was outside my bedroom door; I moved to turn the light switch on and realised I wasn't home at all. My light switch was a square shape but this one was a round, old fashioned one with a flick switch. I turned the light on to see that I was standing at the top of a large staircase. There were large windows to the right of me and the staircase curved down into a reception area. There was a beautiful plush, deep red, carpet that ran along the top landing, down the stairs and into the reception room. I walked down the stairs and there were many people there but I didn't know them. I walked around the corner of the staircase and suddenly I saw my Mum. She was standing there and holding a drink. She looked about fifteen years younger than normal and standing next to her was Robert, her boyfriend who had passed away just after I got married. I hugged him and I was so pleased to see him. We spoke of things he was worried about, things he had not dealt with when he was alive. I told him there was nothing to worry about and it was all taken care of, Robert stood there with tears of relief in his eyes. With that I gave him another hug and said goodbye to him and my Mum and then went back to the bottom of the staircase. There was a large soft seat there and I sat down wondering if I would see Denise. I waited for a while but she didn't show up so I thought I would go home. As soon as I thought that I found myself on the floor of my bedroom. I knew there were two spirits with me but I couldn't see them. I couldn't believe I was on the floor and remember saying, *"Well you might've put me back on my blooming bed."* So I climbed up on the bed and I could feel my body as I laid down into myself. The next moment I was wide awake in bed laying there with Gary snoring quietly next to me. I was so thrilled that I had managed, with Fred's help, to overcome my fear and meet up with Robert and my Mum in the spirit realms. I had many wonderful experiences after that, some with the noises and vibrations and some without. But the fear of the noises and vibrations had gone, well almost anyway. I wasn't 100% happy with it, I put up with it.

Chapter 21
Ben

Ben was born on the 26th November and those who love me in the spirit world were making sure that all went well with the birth. I was taken into hospital on the day that Ben was due to be induced because my blood pressure was high. When my contractions started, I was in the ward and the nurses checked on me and said I wasn't ready to go down to delivery yet. Every time I had a wave of pain it seemed to get longer and longer. Mentally I asked spirit to help me with the pain. Suddenly I was given the vision of a beautiful turquoise sea. There was a huge wave and a surfer on the wave. Every time the contraction pain started, the wave would grow and when the contraction got to its peak, the wave in the vision would curl over and break and the surfer would ride the white surf. All this time I could feel a hand upon my forehead, although I couldn't see anyone there. Then the process would start again, the waves came quicker and then the nurse came up to check me and I was taken down to the delivery room. I gave birth to Ben and Gary and I were so happy, our family was now complete. But a few weeks later I had to spend a night in hospital away from Ben and my family. I had developed a very bad breast abscess and I had to put Ben on bottled milk as it was too painful to feed him. I was taken into hospital to have the abscess cut out. As I drifted off to sleep that night I heard a baby cry. There were no babies in the ward I was in and I just knew it was Ben crying. The next thing I knew I was at home standing over Ben's cot and touching his cheek. I didn't remember anymore until I felt myself flying very fast about 3 feet high above the floors of the hospital corridors. I flew through the doors of my ward and woke up to find myself back in my bed. Ben needed me and even though I was in the hospital, spiritually I was able to be with him. As soon as I held Ben, I knew that he was going to be a spiritual child. Even though Richard and Glen had seen spirit somehow I knew that with Ben it would be stronger.

When Ben was about 4 years old, I brought him home from playschool and he went upstairs to play in his bedroom while I cooked lunch. Richard and Glen were both at school and we were in our house on our own or so I thought. Ben came running down the stairs calling me and I asked him what the matter was, because he sounded worried. He said, "That *man won't stop swinging me around.*" I rushed up into the bedroom and there was no-one around. I checked the other rooms as well, still nobody was there. I asked Ben again what had happened. He said that there was a man in his bedroom who was swinging him around and he didn't like it. I asked Ben what he looked like. Ben described a man who sounded like Robert. I asked Ben what the man was wearing and Ben said he was wearing a jumper with diamonds on it. That convinced me it was Robert as he loved wearing Pringles jumpers and they always had diamond patterns on them. I told Ben that if he saw this man again to tell him that he didn't like being swung round and he wouldn't do it anymore. Ben seemed happy with this and he never mentioned it again. Sometimes when he got a telling off from me, I would often find him sitting on the stairs telling someone that I couldn't see about how rotten I was, bless him. As Ben grew older, he often asked me about heaven and God. He also took a huge interest in the collection of crystals that I had built up. I taught him how different crystals hold different energies that can help us on a healing vibration. Whenever we visited a shop that sold crystals Ben would choose one for me and when I read what the specific crystal was used for it was always appropriate for what I needed at the time. Even though Ben was very young, it seemed as though God had given me someone who understood everything that I was being drawn to. Ben also gave me encouragement where others failed.

Chapter 22
Trance and rescue

My spiritual life was going through a major change and it came one night in a dream. I dreamt that I was back at Mum's home in Croydon. Mum was in the kitchen and I was talking to her. Suddenly I was aware of a Japanese lady standing next to me. She had black hair which was done up on the top of her head with 2 large wooden sticks to keep her hair in place, and she wore a kimono which was cream with a jade and rose pattern all over it. As I spoke to Mum, I felt her move into my body from the side. I could feel every part of her, even her high cheek bones upon my face. The dream faded away and I woke up to find it was 4 o'clock in the morning. The next time I was at church, I mentioned it to a woman called Pat, who I had become very friendly with. Pat told me that the Japanese lady may have been a guide introducing herself to me, and I found this to be true about 3 months later. The beginners circle had closed at church and I felt lost without it. My friend Pat said she ran circles from her home and I could join hers. Pat said that I would have to join the healing circle first as this would enable her to see how developed I was. This was wonderful, they say that when one door closes another one opens and that was exactly what happened. I joined Pat's healing circle which was very similar to the healing circle at church but Pat also included spiritual teachings as well. Each week she would choose a reading from one of her many books and we would take it in turns to read it out. I really enjoyed the spiritual teachings and the ones from Pat's White Eagle books were a firm favourite. Then Pat would lead us into meditation and afterwards we would give each other healing. Sometimes when we were in meditation, I would feel warm hands on my back and my neck. They would be gently massaging me. I would open my eyes expecting to see spirit but I never did, and everyone else would still have their eyes shut. It was the wonderful spirit healers drawing close to me, to help me ease my stiff neck and back. A few months afterwards, Pat said that she could see that I would be ok in her other circle. So I left the healing circle in order to sit in the other one. Pat told me that sometimes people only sat in this circle for a few weeks because some people weren't ready to work so closely with spirit. I was told that if I felt uncomfortable, then I must say so, then I could go back to the other group. There were 6 people in the circle and most did the healing circle as well, so I knew them quite well. I felt really excited although I really didn't know what to expect. The first night I went, we were all sat in Pat's sitting room. The curtains were drawn and the lights were low. Candles had been lit and prayers were said, then we were taken into meditation. After our meditation, we were told to stay in the quiet and invite our spirit guides to draw really close. The room got incredibly warm and I felt a little worried. I could sense movement in the room, quite close to me and I could feel my throat getting uncomfortably dry. Suddenly I had a vision of the desert and I heard, in my mind, a male voice say God bless. He introduced himself to me as Ahmed and he said that when he lived on the Earth plane he prayed to Allah. Ahmed told me that he had been involved in lots of fighting and killing in the name of Allah and now he knew that all his fighting had been in vain because all paths lead to God. He was my life guide and he would be with me, guiding me and looking after me until my time here was completed. I heard Pat speak to me and ask if I had been given anything. I told Pat what Ahmed had told me and she said that I might not always see him but if I felt my throat go dry like that when I was in meditation, I would know that he was with me. I realised that his throat must have felt like that all the time when he lived in the desert. Pat then spoke to another in the group, asking her to speak. Pat was told that she had a rescue, it was a man who had died but had somehow got lost and we were to help him back to the spirit realms. (To the light). As the woman spoke, her voice changed slightly and she started speaking and sounding like a man. The voice of the spirit was coming through her. I started to feel frightened but as soon as I did, I heard Ahmed telling me to keep calm and he told me to send my love to the spirit that was speaking through the woman. I immediately relaxed as I sent my love to him. The man said his name was Jim and he had been in an accident in a car. He said that he couldn't move because he was in pain. Pat told this man that he had died in the accident and that the pain was not there anymore. If he imagined the pain gone it would go. All this time I was sending him love and I had the thought that all the others in the circle were doing the same. Jim said that the pain was going, he couldn't believe it. Pat told him to walk forward and he would see a bright light. She said he mustn't go into the light until he saw someone that he knew. As she said this, with my eyes shut, I could see it was getting lighter and the atmosphere in the room felt lighter as well. Suddenly, in my mind's eye, I saw a door slightly open and just as Jim said he could see a door, I saw it open wide. I saw beautiful white flowers everywhere and the smell of delicate perfume filled the room. Jim then said he could see flowers and he could see the shadow of someone. As the shadow moved closer, he could see it was his Mum and as this happened, I felt a rush of emotion as it suddenly got very bright and Jim went on into the spirit realms with his mother. This was my very first experience of witnessing a soul rescue and I felt so privileged at being part of it. I asked Pat why she told the man to wait until he saw someone he knew. Pat said that some spirits were frightened and she couldn't be sure they would go through if they were on their own. Most spirits go to straight where they are supposed to be, but a few get lost and are guided by the angels to the light that comes from spiritual circles such as the one that I was sitting in. There are also some spirits who are so attached to their material things that they refuse to part with these things, so they stay around their homes and belongings instead of going to where they should be. Of course all of these spirits can only be guided with love. If they refuse to be helped then we send them love and healing just as we would if it were someone on the Earth plane.

Each one of us had turns of speaking about the spirit that was with us and there were lots of teachings that were also given. Again I could feel a wonderful energy with me, the energy felt very gentle and there was almost a fun element to it. I could feel my face taking on a different shape, my cheeks felt strange and I was aware of my cheekbones. I felt extremely happy and my face broke out into a big smile. I felt as though I wanted to speak because I could feel my lips parting. I heard Pat say "To the one who is with Lorraine I invite you to speak." I then felt my mouth open and I said God bless. I was aware that I was speaking and the words were not in my voice. I knew that the Japanese lady, who I dreamt about, was with me and she was speaking through me. She said her name was Jasmine and she was a guide who would help me with my development. She had a sort of sing song voice and she had a great sense of humour. As she spoke, I was very aware that my hands were gently moving. Jasmine told us of her life and she said that she would be with me at the circle, to speak through me to bring teachings to the group. When she had finished speaking I felt her withdraw, but I was very much aware of her for the rest of the evening. When we had all spoken, Pat's guide spoke through her. She was a sister of mercy and she seemed very strict with her teachings. She spoke about protection and the importance of it. This of course we knew but it is always a good thing to be reminded of it. The circle was closed down in prayer and the evening ended. I drove home on a high, I felt so wonderful. I was so pleased to be part of that group and I couldn't believe that a spirit had spoken through me. That was the start of many evenings of spirit speaking through me to the others in the group. We did many rescues and had much laughter and tears with our spirit friends. We got to know the regular spirits who spoke through us and Jasmine was a firm favourite because of her wonderful sense of humour.

A few years after being in Pat's circle, I was asked by my friend, Cathy, if I would run a trance and rescue circle at a hall where I had been teaching in Rochester. I wanted to say yes straight away but my doubt in my abilities stopped me. So I said I would let them know in a month's time. I didn't want to take something on that I wasn't ready for. I knew a couple of people who had done that and had tried to run before they could walk, as they say. Things had gone very wrong for them and I didn't want that to happen to me. That night I had a dream and I dreamt that my friend Bill came to my home. Bill is a man who is straight to the point, and I like that because I know where I am with him. In my dream I was telling him about the offer of running a trance and rescue circle and how I wasn't sure if I could do it. Bill looked me straight in the eyes and said, *"Of course you bloody can."* And with that I woke up. I knew that this was my confirmation that it would be ok.

My own circle started in the January with my group of friends in Rochester. I was really interested in the teachings that spirit brought through at Pat's circle and I hoped that ours would be similar. I didn't really want to do rescues as I hadn't had a lot of experience with that sort of work. But our spirit guides had other ideas and because our circle seemed to be 80% rescue work and 20% teachings. The circle taught us all how important it was to help lost souls. But we also realised how few of these types of circles there are. Also I knew, that if eventually, any of my group were to run spiritual groups, they would know how to help lost souls who may be drawn to them.

Chapter 23
Visitors at Night

One night I was woken up, or so I thought, by movements next to my bed. I say, so I thought, because as I turned over to see what was happening, I realised that I was out of my body. There was a child standing by my bed. He was about 8 years old and he had very dark hair, possibly black. He had the biggest dark brown eyes that held my gaze and I could feel the love coming from this little boy. I sat up on the edge of my bed and started speaking to him. I found that when I spoke to him my voice sounded very muffled but when he spoke I could hear him clearly. I realised that I was trying to speak to him through my mouth as I normally would but as I was out of my body I should have spoken to him telepathically, then the sound would have been clear. I don't remember him telling me his name but I found out that he was Spanish and he told me about his life there. The rest of the details and experience seemed to fade away into a dream until I was woken up by my alarm going off. A few nights later, I opened my eyes again to the feeling of someone pulling on my bed sheets. Back in my younger days I would have been so scared, but now I was used to meeting all sorts of people in my bedroom at night. But what a surprise I had. There, standing at the side of my bed, was a lovely creature. She stood about a metre tall, and she was dressed in a long black skirt with a black top that had short black sleeves. She wore a white apron with a bib and the apron had a frilly edge to it. She had a white frilly cap on her head much like a housemaid would have worn in the Victorian days. She had twinkly eyes and a friendly smile and a snout for a nose, it was similar to a pig's snout but shorter. She was so lovely and I leant forward and put my hands underneath her chin gently and told her she was beautiful. My heart just melted as she spoke in a voice that was as clear and pure as a crystal bell. She told me that her name was Stanton. We spoke but for some reason I never seem to be allowed to remember the conversation. I can only think that maybe I went astral travelling with this creature, perhaps it was to her world.

I have always been an animal lover and I was getting lots of attention from spirit animals at night as well. I often felt my cats that had passed away on the bed and I would feel and hear them purring. So one night when I felt movement on my bed, I put my hand out to feel who it was. Once again I was out of my body when I did this and, expecting to see my cats, I was surprised to see a cat and a dog that hadn't belonged to me. Even now as I write this I feel tears in my eyes because they had been badly neglected and were covered with fleas. The cat was a tabby and the dog was a small poodle. The poodle's eyes were so red and sore. They just wanted to be loved and that's why they had come to me, and that night they were loved, by me and whoever brought them to me. I know that all beings and creatures astral travel in their sleep. I don't know whether these poor animals were alive somewhere on our Earth or whether they had passed away. But the experience upset me quite a lot and I found it hard to think about afterwards without being reduced to tears. Even so, should any other animals who have been cruelly treated be brought to me by spirit I would love them with all my heart.

It wasn't only people I didn't know that I saw at night. One night I woke up at about 3am because I needed to go to the bathroom. When I walked back into the bedroom I saw Gary sitting on the bed. He was facing away from me looking towards the windows. I then realised that Gary was out of his body because I could see his physical body sleeping. I just looked at him and got in bed and went straight to sleep. While I was putting the kettle on in the morning I remembered what I had seen. Why hadn't I spoken to him, telepathically or verbally? I could have kicked myself. What an opportunity I'd missed. The more I thought about it the more annoyed I felt at myself, but then I wanted to tell Gary what I had seen. I knew I shouldn't have said anything to Gary and I was going to keep quiet but it was almost as though I had a little devil on one shoulder and a little angel on the other. The angel was saying don't tell him, don't tell him, and of course you can guess what the devil was saying can't you. Tell him, tell him. Well as Gary came downstairs I couldn't keep quiet any longer, so I told him that I had seen his spirit sitting on the bed that night. He wasn't amused one bit; in fact he said with disgust *"Oh what do you think I'm gonna die or something?"* I told you not to tell him I heard a voice say. I didn't want to upset him; I suppose I just wanted him at the least to believe and at the most to be interested. I was still finding it very hard that I wasn't able to share my most wonderful experiences with my husband. It seemed to me that I was having this whole other life that he knew nothing about and that made me very sad. But the following day I found I had someone else in my life that needed to hear about my night time visitors. I had been doing a weekend cleaning job at the local working men's club and a woman started there as a cleaner a few months before. Her name was Diane and we hit it off from the first time she started there. Although we had never met before there seemed to be some sort of connection, and a very boring cleaning job turned into a wonderful time of chat, laughter and cleaning. We talked about anything and everything and one day she mentioned that she thought there was someone in her bedroom watching her while she was asleep. I told her about the spirits that draw close to us when we are worried and that I felt it was her grandmother watching over her. Diane said that she did believe in spirits and that there was a lot going on in her life emotionally. I told her to talk to her gran as though she was still on the Earth and then her gran would know that she was aware of her. That would give both of them comfort. Diane asked me if I saw any spirits, I told her about some of them and then I found myself talking about my visit from the creature called Stanton. As I was speaking about her I was thinking I shouldn't be telling her this because she is going to think I am crazy. But when I had finished Diane said that was wonderful. Then she said that when she was a child she used to see little pixies in her bedroom at night. They carried musical instruments and some played them. She used to watch them walk across her bedroom floor and under her bed and then disappear. Diane had never told anyone about this and I felt that this was a relief to finally talk about it. It seems so sad that sometimes in our lives we go through things that are so acceptable as a child but as we grow up it gets pushed into the darkness because we have no-one to talk to. Children are our future and one of the most important things I think the best thing we can do, is that when they tell us they have seen something unbelievable, is to be open minded and supportive. Just because we, as adults, don't understand it, it doesn't mean it doesn't exist.

It was a Sunday morning a few months later when I was to have another experience with my red skinned alien. I was asleep and having a very strange dream. I dreamt that I was sitting at a large rectangular wooden table. There were about 5 other people sitting around it with me. There was a woman at the head of the table and I knew her. She was one of the mediums who served at the church I belonged to. She looked at me and she seemed to dissolve down into two bright orbs of light and then the lights moved across the table towards me. They stopped in front of me and I heard a voice saying to me that I had great power and I must learn how to use it. The table and all the people then disappeared. And I found myself standing with my Mum in front of a large building on a busy London street. We walked into the building and across to a waiting lift. We both got in and I pressed the button for the sixteenth floor. The lift started moving very quickly but it was moving in a diagonal direction. The lift stopped and Mum and I got out. Mum waited by the lift while I walked into what looked like a large classroom. There were several people there, all strangers and it seemed that we were waiting for a teacher. I sat down and suddenly I felt myself changing. I could feel a ridge coming across my forehead; it was protruding quite a bit. My hands had changed into the long fingered hands with the claws and my whole body had changed. I was the red skinned alien. I was sitting on a chair and I noticed a girl on the other side of the room. As I looked across to her I saw her skin drop away as though she were letting a dress fall to the floor. She was a male red skinned alien, the same as I was. I got up and walked over to her. I saw that we were both wearing a large combat belt with a gun attached to it. We had no tops on and were both very muscular. There was a thick strap that ran across one shoulder down to the belt on our waists. I felt very military, if that makes sense. We embraced and in a deep masculine voice I called him my friend. Then suddenly I found myself back in my bed taking a huge breath that left me feeling shocked. My heart was thumping hard and it took me a few minutes to calm down. I looked at the time and saw that the alarm was nearly due to go off. I got out of bed and went downstairs. I went straight into the kitchen and put the kettle under the tap to make a cup of tea. As I did this, I felt tears streaming down my face as I sobbed, crying out that I wanted my friend. I felt distraught, like part of me had died. I sat on the armchair and sobbed for about half an hour. I felt so empty and so alone, and as I write this now my throat is tightening up and the feeling is returning, with tears again in my eyes I'm thankful that Gary has just gone out. Part of me was, and still is, missing and even though I have much love in my family and friends I pray to God that I may find my friend again in this lifetime. I had to somehow push that experience to the back of my mind as I went to my cleaning job that day. I couldn't tell my friend Diane about it as I felt too raw inside. Over the following weeks, I seemed to get back to some normality but every spare moment I had I was searching on the internet and in books for more information. This did open up a lot more questions than answers for me. Although I found out a lot of information about aliens, nothing I read or saw seemed to fit what I had been in the dream. One day, as I was just about to order another book on alien's, spirit gently but firmly told me to stop searching, and I did Now I wait patiently for more to be given to me if and when I am ready.

Chapter 24
Love overcomes all

At Ben's playschool, I met a young woman called Angela. She had the most beautiful face and skin that looked like porcelain. She had long, dark curly hair and a mischievous smile. She had a heart of gold and would help anybody out if she could. I had mentioned to her about healing as she had been suffering with emotional problems, and she said she would think about it. A week later, Angela told me that although she liked the thought of having healing she felt very frightened. But her Mum Julie would love healing as she was suffering as well. It was arranged that her Mum would come to my home and have healing and Angela would just sit in the armchair and watch. This made me smile because I knew Angela would still receive the healing energies while in the room. They both came round one Tuesday morning and Julie sat on the stool while Angela sat in the armchair. I opened up in prayer and started to give Julie healing. She was very nervous and I could feel her shaking beneath my hands. I asked her if she would like me to stop but she said no carry on. Spirit was telling me that Julie was an old soul which meant that she had lived on the Earth many times before. They also said that she was very advanced spiritually and this puzzled me as the nervousness I felt suggested the opposite. I carried on with the healing and when I had finished I went to get Julie a glass of water. I asked Angela if she was ok, only to find that she had fallen asleep. The healing energy had certainly got to Angela, but Julie was still nervous. Then it all came pouring out. She told me that there was a spirit of a man in her home. He was a very bad spirit and he would throw things around. He would swear and take knives out of the kitchen drawer and throw them across the room. Julie was staying at Angela's home at the time because she was too frightened to stay at home. Her husband worked nights and the spirit was quite quiet during the day but at night he was a menace. It made sense how Julie was when I was giving her healing. She was scared stiff and who could blame her. It was like something out of a horror film. I felt worried myself I must admit but I knew I had to help her or find someone who could. I immediately asked my guide if we could help. He said that I was to invoke Archangel Michael and ask him to put his blue light around her. I did this and Julie said that she had moved lots of times and every house that she had moved into was badly haunted. I realised then that the spirit was connected to her and not to her home. My guide showed me a picture of a Ouija board and then a picture of Julie when she was small but afterwards it had been put in the shed. This was where her problems had started. The spirit had been allowed to come through and attach itself to Julie. But then my guide said that even though Julie was new to healing the fact was that this was a spiritual test for her as she was an old soul. He said that provided Julie was in agreement, she was to have several sessions of healing, which would then enable her natural courage and strength to deal with the situation. It was a test of spiritual faith for her as the first thing that she had to learn to do was to send the spirit love and healing. My guide said that as soon as Julie had started her healing session's things would change. The spirit would get noisier and more troublesome and this was because he would see the light coming through her. He would know that as her light shone brighter he would lose his hold over her. The reason Julie had to learn to pray for him was because his terror and rampage was born out of his own fear. He was lost and unloved and, as much as Julie needed healing so did the spirit that was haunting her. While I was giving her healing I saw a priest in my mind's eye walking around both of us sprinkling holy water. The following week Julie came for healing and told me that as she walked back into her home after the first healing session, she heard a tremendous bang in her kitchen. She could sense the spirits rage as she moved around the house. He got so angry and violent that she packed her bag and moved in with Angela for the week. She told me that she had also found it very hard to pray for the spirit but again I told her it was all part of her test. It was of course her choice but it was the right thing to do. After three healing sessions, Julie felt strong enough to move back into her home. After all, she loved her home and didn't want to give it up. She found the strength to pray for him and she sent the spirit healing thoughts. It was, as they say, a battle of the wills between her and the spirit. He was still very noisy but something had changed because he wasn't as violent. Over the weeks, Julie sensed him watching her but all the time growing quieter, just the odd noise here and there. Then one day, as Julie returned home from work she knew before she walked in through the door that he had gone. Her home was at last peaceful and she was able to get a good night's sleep. Julie came back to me for one last healing session, bringing me a beautiful little cross on a chain. She told me that she was still praying for the spirit wherever he was, and she understood why she had to go through that experience, as frightening as it was. It doesn't always occur to pray for those who we would describe as evil, but evil is born out of fear and to strip away the fear we must give love. Love is a light in the darkness and it will change your lives forever.

The healing and guidance that Julie received from spirit had helped Angela so much. She began to take a deeper interest in spiritual things and was always asking questions, which led to many evenings of laughter and teachings. She, like her Mum, also had a natural ability to sense spirit which led to a very interesting evening. I went around there one evening for a glass of wine and a chat, and Angela asked me if I could sense anything up on her landing. She said that it quite often felt cold there and she didn't like it. Also her youngest boy Rowan was having trouble sleeping in his bedroom. Rowan was the same age as Ben and they were friends at school. Well I went up to their landing but I couldn't sense anything there. But I could understand her feeling that way after everything that her Mum had gone through. I told her that I would open myself up to spirit and see if I could get any information for her. As soon as I did this, a cool draft came into the living room and rested in front of us. I sensed a little boy and he said his name was Andrew. He said that he liked Angela because of her energy. He said that she reminded him of yellow. I could totally understand what he meant because if I had to call her a colour that would have been it. Despite many problems she always came across to me as happy and fun, just like sunshine. Then I heard a little girl's voice call Mummy. I asked Angela if she had had a miscarriage. She said she had and it was a few years beforehand. The little girl told me that her name was Sophie. They asked if they could sit on Angela's lap and Angela agreed as long as she didn't see them, because, although they were children, she still felt a little scared. But she didn't mind them being there now as she knew who they were. I felt them move up onto Angela's lap. It felt like a soft cool breeze and then we could both feel the cool energy all over her lap. I saw Andrew rest his head upon Angela's chest. There was a tall slender spirit that appeared by the living room door. It was a woman who looked after them and she told us that she was the children's guardian. These spirit children played with Angela's son Rowan when he was asleep. When he slept, he would come out of his body and play with the spirit children. This is quite normal and most of the time our children don't remember doing it. But sometimes they arrived before he had fallen asleep properly and he sensed their energy. This is what was frightening him. While we were talking, I noticed that Angela's hand had come up to her lap as though she were putting it there for support. They had a little brown and white dog with them that came to Rowans bedroom as well. Andrew told me that when he was on the Earth plane he couldn't talk properly. He had a stutter and was bullied because of it. He hated school and Rowan was also having problems at school and I think that Andrew was friends with Rowan because of the similar problems. The guardian of the children said that they had to go and when I looked at my watch I could see that it was nearly midnight. As the children and the guardian left, the room got warmer. Angela and I felt so happy and I knew that she was looking forward to feeling the coolness on the landing again. She said the next time she'll say hello to them.

My faith in those who guide me and help me along my pathway grow stronger and stronger but I try never to take anything for granted. It's easy to become complacent about protection when you get used to seeing and hearing spirit around you. So when I was asked by a friend and neighbour of mine if I would go to a pub where she worked, to help with a troublesome spirit, I immediately prayed to God and asked if it was safe for me to do so. There are so many different energies around that I will never place myself in a situation without the agreement and protection of my angels and guides.

The pub was called The Red Deer and it was opposite the working men's club where I had my cleaning job. My friend had told me that one evening, while the pub was open to customers, the door by the bar burst open and there was a rush of air along the bar. All the customers felt it and then the door that led out into the street opened and slammed shut. The door by the bar led down to the cellars and quite often the barrels would be moved on their own. Also other things down there would be moved when no-one was there. The lights upstairs would also flicker on and off, my friend and the staff who worked there weren't frightened just very curious as to what was going on. Before I went down there, I prayed and asked for the protection from my angel and Archangel Michael and I heard spirit telling me not to worry, I would be safe. I went into the pub which was closed to customers as it was early in the morning and sat at the bar. I opened myself up to spirit and waited. I couldn't sense anything and I was beginning to feel a little awkward. I didn't want the people who worked there to think I was unable to pick anything up. But the words 'have faith' came to me. My friend suggested that I go through the door and down into the basement. I wanted to go but I felt so worried. I hadn't done anything like this before and, quite frankly, I felt a little scared. But again I heard 'have faith'. I walked down the stairs and at the bottom was the door that led to the first cellar. I stood by the door and slowly pushed it open as my friend turned the light on. The cellar was cold, still and empty. I walked in and felt nothing, nothing at all. I was relieved but as my friend and landlady were watching me expectantly, I felt like a fake. There was another cellar and the landlady said this was where most of the things happened. I put my hand on the handle to open the door and as I did this, I found myself saying "I come in love and in the name of God I will help you." The door opened into darkness and I walked in closely followed by the others. I felt the air become very cold and again, I repeated "I come in love, and in the name of God I will help you." Suddenly I felt a rush of air beside me and my body tingled all over. I felt immensely sad and a wave of emotion washed over me. A male energy kept repeating "This is my home, this is where I belong." Then I saw him. The gentleman was beside himself with tears. It was all I could do to stop the tears streaming down my cheeks as I tried to calm him down. It was pure emotion and somehow I had to calm him down or his emotions would have affected me so badly that I wouldn't have been able to help him as I would have been too upset to cope with the energy. I kept reassuring him that he would be ok over and over again. Eventually he calmed down enough to speak to me. I was then clairvoyantly shown mattresses on the floor and I knew that this room was his sleeping quarters. He told me that he was upset at what was going to happen to the pub. I had found out that the pub was due to close down at the end of the week, and eventually the whole block was going to be knocked down. He was upset and frustrated because he hadn't been able to voice his views. Nobody could hear him and he hadn't meant to upset anyone when he flew through the bar room. It wasn't rage, it was just pure frustration as he slammed the door. He said that his name was Joe and he lived downstairs and only went upstairs for work purposes. He gave the name of Peg, Frieda and a few others, some of which were recognized by the landlady as she had delved into the history of the pub beforehand. After reassuring Joe it was ok, we went upstairs and Joe came with us. He said there used to be a distillery there and an old hospital along the road. He spoke of a fishmonger in Strood that was connected to his family. He gave the year of 1826 and he told us that if we thought that Strood was busy now, in those days it was chaos. There was something happening around every corner. As he was giving this information to me it seemed that his memories were flowing through my mind as though I were watching a film reel. I had to find out whether Joe was stuck on the Earth plane and needed help getting to the light. Joe said he wasn't stuck there, he had chosen to stay because that was his life and where he belonged. It may have been a hard life but he loved every minute of it. Even though his wife had passed over many years ago and had gone to the light, Joe was quite happy to stay here. I told him that he didn't have to stay there. He could go to his family and take his memories with him, nothing could take those away. The life he was trying to live was all memories. He told me that he was exhausted and I could feel that as well. Joe said that he would go because his wife was waiting for him. He told me that he wouldn't give the landlady any more problems and after a quiet goodbye he left. I came home and cleansed myself with white light and thanked my angels for the help they gave. The next day, I was walking down the road to my cleaning job and I walked past the pub. Out of the side of my eye I saw Joe sitting by the window and he was smiling at me. Then he waved goodbye and vanished. I spoke to my neighbour a week later and she said that all the noise and disturbances had stopped. I felt so happy that I had been able to help that dear soul move on.

Chapter 25
Psychic Attack

At my church, I had made many friends and things were going very well for me. But one day a woman joined our church and things started to change. I got on very well with most people and it was unusual for me not to like someone. I found it very easy to focus on their positive energy, even if others thought there was something wrong with them. But with this woman it was very difficult. Normally I would keep my distance if I came across things like this but everywhere I was she seemed to be. I had a thought that at some time in a past life she was connected to black magic. This was somehow confirmed to me by a gentleman in our church, who was the nicest person I had ever met. He was like an angel and he had never said anything negative about anyone in all the years I had known him. He told me that as she walked into our church he had a sense of pure evil. I knew she was in need of healing and I included her in my nightly prayers, but that was all I did. I started to feel very uncomfortable around her and I would double the strength of my protection. Then one night I dreamt of her. She and I were standing facing each other with about a metre between us. I could feel a huge amount of energy coming off of her towards me and vice versa. It was like two magnets repelling each other. The dream only seemed to last for a couple of minutes but it was the first thing I remembered when I woke up. I didn't feel frightened about it but I knew it meant something significant. Two nights later I was asleep in my bed and I heard the bedroom door slam open as though someone had come through it in a rage. Then I felt the weight of somebody upon me. They were rubbing my third eye and doing it harder and harder until it started to hurt. I shouted out for them to stop but they just did it harder. I struggled to lift my arm up under the weight but I managed to do so, and I felt somebody's hand and fingers clamped to my forehead. With all the strength I could muster, I peeled the fingers away from me. I hadn't realised that I was out of my body until I saw myself from above giving somebody a huge telling off. I couldn't see who it was but I had my suspicions. The next thing I knew was that I was awake and back in my bed. Gary was fast asleep next to me; I didn't wake him up but got up and went to the bathroom. I could still feel the burning on my forehead so I looked in the mirror. My forehead had a round red mark on it about the size of a golf ball. I got back into bed but I couldn't settle so I went downstairs. I wasn't frightened which absolutely amazed me but of course my mind was in overdrive. I spent about 3 hours downstairs and then went back up to bed. The next day I phoned the president of my church and also one of my friends. They both suggested that I had experienced a psychic attack. This felt right but I couldn't understand why, as I knew I had protected myself well. Suddenly the dream I had about the woman at the church came back to me. I knew that it was her who had attacked me, and then I wondered if my protection hadn't been strong enough. That following night, as I prepared for bed, I lit a candle. I said my prayers and asked Archangel Michael and my guardian angel to surround me in their blue light. Even though the experience hadn't frightened me, I certainly didn't want to go through it again. That night I found myself out of my body again. This time I was looking down at myself sleeping peacefully, surrounded by a beautiful blue light. I know that the angels were showing me my protection was working. At church things started to get back to normal. The woman was going there less and less until one day she just stopped going altogether. I have dreamt about her several times since then but the dreams have always been good. I often find that in my dreams we are smiling and laughing together. About 6 months later, I was teaching up at a hall in Rochester and I was telling the story of what I had gone through. Again I was teaching about protection and as I spoke to the group there, my guide told me that it had been a spiritual test and I had passed with flying colours. That made me smile and I thought spiritually I must have known it was going to happen. I must have been forewarned, which was why I hadn't been frightened. They say that people come into your life for different reasons and I now know why I had to encounter that woman into my life.

I have been going to see a woman who is an osteopath; she also does cranial and sacral therapy. She is a very spiritual person and understands a lot of what I was being drawn to. We have had many wonderful conversations while she was giving me my treatment on my back. One day I happened to mention the psychic attack that I had dealt with and the negativity that had surrounded me then. She told me that she had an instrument that worked by violet light and it could be used to cleanse people of negative energies that had attached to the aura. She would use this instrument on me to see if I needed to be freed of anything. As I was walking to my appointment I was thinking about my protection. Then I was shown a picture in my mind of a beautiful blue diamond. I was told that it was my spiritual protection now, because my protection had been upgraded. When I got to my appointment, I was told to lie down on the healing bed. I had to lay face down with my head in a hole on the bed. She turned the instrument on with the violet ray and started to run it gently over my back. She told me that I should be as relaxed as possible and could I go into meditation. I laughed, how on Earth I was going to be able to meditate in that position. Still, no sooner had I thought that I had a vision of myself swimming in a beautiful deep pool that was surrounded by rocks. There was a beautiful waterfall in front of me. As I swam I looked up to see brilliant blue sky and trees all around me. Suddenly I was shown two jagged pieces of slate which were very sharp. I knew that they were in my back and they were wedged under my left shoulder blade. About 30 seconds after that thought, I felt my osteopath put the violet ray instrument at that very spot. She held it there for quite a while. Still I had my eyes shut and then I saw a long box. The lid opened and a grotesque fat man climbed out of it. I couldn't see his face but it felt to me like he was some sort of clown. I had the thought that it was symbolic of the negativity and fear for the person who had been sending me bad thoughts. After that it felt like I was levitating a few inches of off the bed and I was gently moving backwards and forwards. It was such a pleasant feeling I had trouble keeping awake. My osteopath didn't know what I had seen, but she told me that she had drawn the person out of me and put her in a cage where she could do no more harm. Then she laid me on my back and put the violet ray machine on my third eye to draw out the negativity there. I had my eyes open and I felt all warm and tingly, as though I were being wrapped in the softest cotton wool. When she had finished, I thanked her and went home. I felt exhausted but I knew that everything bad had been taken away from my aura because of what I had been shown. At some point that night, spirit told me that I was up to full power again. I said my prayers of gratitude and healing and thanked God for bringing my osteopath friend into my life.

I had been thinking about the sharp pieces of slate in my back, and I was given the thought that as the energy of these thoughts had come to me, they had got stuck in my aura which then caused me tremendous back pain. I had always known that negative thoughts were bad for you, as I expect most people know. But I didn't realise, until that point, that what we send out to other people is so powerful that it can manifest in all sorts of ways. What's more, when you send out a negative or positive thought to someone it comes back to you big time. Because we live in a world where everything is energy and the energy is vibrating, nothing stands still, even time. So eventually, like the ripples on a pond, the energy that we send out will return to us. The positive energy we send out will return in the most wonderful ways, bringing joy and happiness. But the negative energy we send out will bring us pain. Physical and emotional pain that is quite unnecessary for our growth.

Chapter 26
The Violet Flame

I had come to a point in my life where things seemed to be slowing down. Although I was teaching at my church, my other circles had stopped. The services that I was doing at other churches seemed to be slowing down as well, and although I was feeling frustrated at this I didn't seem to have the energy or the inclination to do anything about it. The books that I was starting to be drawn to were about ancient teachings and things that were very confusing to me. I was being drawn into a world that I didn't understand and I had no idea why. Then one night I had a beautiful dream. I was walking down a dusty dirt track and the sun was low, spreading a beautiful golden light around all around me. There were low hedges to my right and a huge house with a wooden veranda to my left. Just as I was walking past the house something made me turn around. There was an elderly man just coming out of his front door. He was very slim, quite tall and oriental looking. I walked up to him and he looked at me and smiled. His face was weathered by the sun and his eyes sparkled with knowledge. His thin wispy hair was moving in the breeze. He was wearing trousers and a checked shirt which looked very old and grubby. But on his feet were the brightest emerald green slippers I had ever seen. He invited me into his home and it was huge. There were rooms, stairways and corridors going off in every direction. The sun was trying very hard to filter through the grime on the windows and there was a thick layer of dust over everything. Absolutely everywhere was piled with old books on every subject you could imagine. Amongst the piles of books were drawings and pictures which seemed to be done in pencils and pastels. The rooms were a dull yellow with faded red beams across the ceilings. Despite the mess, I could tell the gentleman was extremely happy and kind. As I walked through his home, I looked out of the windows at the back of his house, which were a lot clearer to see out of than the front ones. I looked out onto beautiful rolling fields of golden corn and a wispy blue sky. A cat appeared in the room and it reminded me of one of my tabbies. He picked up the cat and it purred loudly in his arms. He told me that he was going to help me understand what I needed to learn. He said that the books represented knowledge and then I realised that the beautiful colour of his slippers represented knowledge as well. Emerald green is often given in spiritual messages to represent knowledge and spiritual growth, I awoke from my dream and I felt a wonderful sense of peace. The frustration I was feeling had left me and I knew that my slowing down was not because I was coming to a stop but because my spiritual learning was changing direction.

One day not long after that dream, I came upon a book called The Emerald Tablets. I was constantly being drawn to this book. Every time I was on the computer researching or reading about different spiritual practises that book was always mentioned, and even though I had never heard of it or knew what it was about, I knew I had to read it. It is a book of ancient teachings written about Thoth, an Atlantean priest king. It brought into my life a greater understanding of how the universe works on a spiritual level and the wisdom that comes with this. I mention this book because it opened up a huge doorway to me and a much deeper understanding of all that exists. I have many more books now on ancient knowledge and some of them make sense but others I am struggling with, but they all have a place in my much crowded home. My bedroom is starting to look like the home of the gentleman guide with the books piled up where ever I can find space.

Books have always played a big part in my life, right from when I was at school, even though, as I said before, I was never academic. Even when I left school and started work, you would always find me in Croydon library in my lunch hour. So it was no surprise that, when I first got involved with the spiritual church, I was buying books on all sorts of spiritual subjects and people. But I found that as I progressed with my spiritual pathway I was losing interest in them. I bought many books but they just sat on my shelves unread. Then one day a medium told me that books were ok for a while but I had to find my own way from my own spiritual experiences. I understood why he told me that because many things I had read, I really wanted to happen to me. I secretly wanted it so much that it was spoiling my own pathway. I was forgetting that it was other people's experiences I was reading, and everybody has a different pathway. So you can never force this pathway, it must happen naturally at your own pace and not at someone else's. So I suppose it must have been a good ten years before I started reading spiritual books again. In a spiritual catalogue that I had started receiving there was a book that I kept being drawn to. Much like The Emerald Tablets I had no idea what it was about. I would find that as I browsed through the catalogue I would always stop at the page it was on, so I thought there must be some reason I needed to read this book. I ordered it and within a couple of weeks it was lying on my table. It was a book all about the violet flame. I had never heard of this before and it spoke about the ascended masters which I knew very little about. As I started to read this book I was aware of a lot of spirits sitting on my sofa next to me. Although I couldn't see them properly I could feel excitement coming from them and I couldn't understand why. I found out that the violet flame is a gift that was given to mankind to help us transmute negative energy into positive energy and light. It will transmute the energy in ourselves as well as the energy all around us. It also said that the violet flame could transmute energy that had been brought through from past lives and this would reduce the need for karmic lessons. The ascended master who looks after the violet flame and distributes it where it's needed, is called Saint Germain. To invoke this violet flame you had to say a rhyme over and over again and the energy and thought of this brought the flame into being. There were lots of rhymes or invocations, and me being a simple soul chose the easiest one to remember. I don't usually go trying things without doing research on them, but it was almost as though I could feel spirit urging me on.

The rhyme was, I am a being of violet fire, and I am the purity God desires. I said a prayer of protection first. Then over and over again I said the rhyme out loud, thinking that it was a good job I was in the house alone or my family would think I was mad. The book suggested that I repeat the rhyme for a minimum of twenty times. Well I got about halfway through and I started to feel very emotional. By the time I got to the twentieth time I had tears streaming down my cheeks and I had to stop. I couldn't believe it. Where on Earth had that come from? I had felt perfectly happy when I started to say the rhyme. I put the book away and washed my face in cold water. I felt really stupid and suddenly very tired so I went up to bed for a nap. The next day after the children went to school I decided to try the violet flame again. I managed to do this without tears this time and managed to repeat the rhyme for about 15 minutes. While I did this and I had my eyes closed and the most beautiful purple light came into my mind. I had seen purple in the past many times but this was far more intense. Later that day as I was looking in the mirror getting ready to go out, I saw myself as a woman of about 20 years older than what I was then. My hair was pulled back into a tight bun and even though I recognised my face it wasn't at all like I am now. I had a harsh look on my face and although I was the same height I was very much larger than I am now. I didn't like what I saw at all and the words that came to me were that I didn't put myself out for anyone and I was a thoroughly nasty person. Then the vision changed, I saw myself as a young boy of about 7 years old. I saw a metal brace on my left leg and I actually felt the underneath of the brace slip under my heel. Then the vision ended and I thought that perhaps that's why I do what I do now, to make up for not helping others before. As for my leg, I have extremely bad varicose veins in both my legs but the left is far worse. Could the effects of the leg brace in a past life have affected my leg in this one? I would never have believed it if I hadn't seen it but that seemed to be the case. I carried on doing my violet flame regularly, and after a particular busy day I felt extremely tired. I thought I would lie on the sofa for a short while and close my eyes. As I was lying there with my eyes closed I saw a white mist develop and it seemed about a metre above my head. Within the mist was a beautiful image. It was oval in shape and it was spinning. It was silver with shafts of coloured lights coming off it in all directions. It had a sort of lattice work pattern to it. It was absolutely beautiful. The colours reminded me of the pretty foil wrapping paper you can get. I had no idea what it meant and I had never seen anything like it before. But that night I was to see it again. I went up to bed feeling like I had been given a sleeping drug, and I must have fallen asleep as soon as my head hit the pillow.

In the night I was aware of a gentle humming noise and it woke me up. The oval spinning image was all around me. It was as though I was inside it. It was huge and it was spinning so fast that it was making me feel dizzy and sick. I shouted out stop and it vanished. The bedroom was quiet and I was alone. I could feel my heart beating and I closed my eyes and went back to sleep. The next day I was thinking about what I had seen. I asked one or two people but nobody could tell me what it was. I didn't mention it to anyone else but I felt that I had opened up other spiritual energies within me, with the aid of the violet flame. As with most things in my life, my daily meditations with the violet flame got less and less, but every so often I would repeat the exercise. Then one night I had the strangest dream. I dreamt that I was in Rochester High Street, and who should I bump into but our Queen. She smiled at me and we went into a large building and into a very beautiful room. The Queen asked me to wait as she went to get something. When she came back she handed me a beautiful pair of violet gloves and a violet handbag that matched. We hugged and I left to find the alarm waking me up out of my dream. I felt so happy and I know that people may say it was only a dream but I knew it had a special meaning. That my violet flame was still working even though I wasn't doing it every day, and that's what spirit did. They gave me the proof every few months that it was still working. About 9 months later I was told by spirit that I would have previous lives shown to me. The next day as I lay in my bed, I started dreaming. I was a man of about seventy years old. I was walking along a side street and suddenly there was a girl of about twelve years old walking past me. As she walked past me I thought of bad things that I would do with her. Suddenly I woke up and I was shocked because I knew that I had been that man. I pushed the dream to the back of my mind and tried to forget it. Three nights later I was having a terrible night. I had woken up at about 2 in the morning and I just couldn't sleep. I got up and went downstairs for a few hours. As it started to get light, I started to get tired so I went back to bed. As soon as I went to sleep I was aware that I was a baby boy of about 6 months old. I was lying on my stomach in my cot. I could see a pink painted wall and I knew I was in a children's home. I heard footsteps come into the *room* and I heard a woman's voice echo, *"What are you doing? You filthy boy."* From next to me I heard a boy cheekily say *"Just fiddling miss."* The dream ended and I woke up. My head felt strange like I had come out of a very long sleep. The final stage of the previous life happened two days later. Again I dreamt I was in the same children's home, in the same cot. But this time I was about 4 years old, and the boy who had been in the next bed to me was now abusing me. I could feel the motion of everything that was happening, but I wasn't afraid because it seemed to me that it was what I had been used to from this boy. The dream ended and I woke up and sat up in bed. I had been shown a life which at first revolted me, but then as it unfolded a great understanding came to me. The feelings that had arisen in the first dream faded away like a gentle breeze and a feeling of acceptance came from deep within.

My next vision brought on by the violet flame was totally different. I was aware of the sound of the sea and beautiful turquoise colours around me. I could feel the warm sun on my face and I suddenly saw myself. I was slim and my hair was long and dark blue, I also had aqua coloured skin. The vision ended and I also heard a voice say Lemurian connections. I opened my eyes and stared at the ceiling. I had never heard of Lemuria so I went to our computer and looked it up. I found out that Lemuria was around at the same time as Atlantis. This was really exciting for me as I really wanted to believe in Atlantis, but until had proof I couldn't believe it just because I had read it was true. I did more research on Lemuria and its civilisation. On one wonderful site I read that the ancient Lemurians had aqua coloured skin which changed to a deeper blue according to the seasons. Also I read somewhere that these ancient people had transparent roofs so that they could see the stars. Well you might say that this was no proof at all, but to me it meant something because there had been so many times in my life when I had said to Gary that I wished that we had a glass roof so we could see the stars. But that wasn't the end of my past life experiences. I woke up one day to find I was a young boy of about ten years old. I heard a woman call me and tell me to get up for school. She spoke in a language to me that was totally different from English and I answered in the same language. I feel that we were speaking Polish but I'm not sure. I jumped out of my bed and hurriedly got dressed. With no time to eat, I grabbed a hat and coat, a school bag and opened a door that led outside. I could hear dogs barking and the air was cold with thick snow on the ground. The vision ended and I was back in my own bed. It seemed that the violet flame had opened up a wonderful doorway into the mysteries of past lives. I must admit that up until that time past lives were something I rarely thought about.

Chapter 27
Astral Rescues and healing

I woke up one morning after a really horrible dream. I dreamt that I was on a train and it was very crowded, a seat became available and I sat down. There were people in the seat opposite me and I was trying to explain to them how the violet flame worked. A small fire appeared in the middle of our compartment, and as I was saying the rhyme of the violet flame, the orange flames turned violet. Then I found, as I was trying to repeat the rhyme, it was getting harder and harder to say. All of a sudden I was in a large room, in the middle of a mass of writhing bodies. Everyone was naked apart from me and I could see my Mum standing at a distance watching me. It was horrible, the sweat, the heat and I could taste blood. I woke up to hear myself saying the violet flame quietly and then the alarm went off. I got up and went downstairs to put the kettle on and start breakfast. My stomach felt horrible as though I had a stomach bug and my head felt muzzy. I couldn't eat breakfast so I just had a cup of tea and a glass of water. I said my prayers and did my protection before I walked to the school with Ben. As I was walking up to school I was aware of a spirit walking with us. Out of the corner of my eye I saw brown shoes and the bottom half of brown trousers. I felt it was one of my grandfathers and as I left Ben at school I saw it again. I could feel the warm energy on my cheek as I walked back home. My mind was on what had happened that night and I was worried that I had forgotten to protect myself the day before. I asked my grandfather whether this was the case. He said that I had been on a rescue mission on the lower spiritual realms. He told me that I had picked up residue of the negative energy that I had been dealing with. My grandfather told me to go home and lie on my bed. I had to put one hand on my stomach and the other hand on my forehead. I was to lay there for about thirty minutes and then have a glass of water. I did this and both of my hands went very warm and started to tingle. I would have fallen asleep if it wasn't for the fact that holding my hand on my forehead was starting to make my arm ache. But after thirty minutes I got up and thanked my spirit helpers, I felt so much better. I felt wonderful as though I had had a thoroughly good spring clean, and really that's exactly what it was. Some weeks later, again while I was sleeping at night, I was aware of a gentle lifting sensation and I thought, here we go again. This was happening on such a regular basis that I was used to it by now... I felt myself flying through the astral realm and it was very dark. Then I heard a movement of heavy chains and I heard a man shouting and swearing at me. I couldn't see anything but I was standing still and I knew that I wasn't on my own. I said that I supposed that this must be hell, and a gentle voice said to me, "There is no such place as hell; it is just a state of mind." And with that we moved away and I woke up in my bed. I knew that when we astral travel we are never alone, and again I knew that I was involved with trying to help poor souls move out of the darkness into the light. Just like the people on our Earth the souls of those who pass away have freewill. Not everyone appreciates the fact that we are trying to help them, if they don't want to listen or go to the light that is their choice. But they are never forgotten and with constant prayers and healing from the angels, they are helped eventually into the light. They are then given spiritual counselling to help them come to terms with what happened in their Earth life. It seems that I have been trained on the Earth, and also in the spirit realms, for rescuing souls, and for that I feel really privileged. Rescue work and healing work is quite often the same thing in a spiritual sense. When we give healing we are quite often rescuing that person from despair and this was the case of another nightly excursion. I found myself astral travelling to a large complex rather similar to the huge shopping malls you get in America. I walked into a cafeteria and there was a young man of about twenty years old. He looked at me and his eyes were blazing. He was so angry and he was swearing and cursing me. Somehow I knew that even though he was doing this he wanted me to help him. As he stood there shouting, I put my hand on the top of his head and I started to invoke the violet flame. I knew that the young man had been taken over by a demon. Over and over I said the rhyme getting louder each time. I could feel the power of the flame building up around the two of us and suddenly it came to a climax and the demon left the young man. The man looked at me and he was dazed, I held both of his hands and continued to give him healing. I didn't need to speak, I just held him. Then I felt a huge wave of divine love come from the man to me. No words were spoken, they didn't need to be. The feeling of love was all that was needed, and that's really what life is all about. Releasing things that should never be there, the things that stop our love which is God's love shine through.

Chapter 28
Angels everywhere

Although I knew angels existed, I had never had much to do with them, not that I recalled anyway. My Mum had seen an angel in her bedroom years ago and seeing the angel had frightened her because she didn't know why it was there. But one day a friend of mine said I was going to work with angels and this surprised me as I knew very little about them. Then that Christmas, a good friend of mine gave me a book on angels. He had never brought me anything like that before and it seemed that I was being pointed in that direction by my spirit friends. I had heard that angels leave signs around that they are with you. They leave white feathers, make beautiful music and you can hear twinkly bell like sounds and I'm sure there are many, many more things that they do to show that they are near us.

It was a hot sunny day and far too hot for me to sit in my garden, so I relaxed lying on the sofa. I struggled to keep my eyes open and eventually gave in to a nap. Then I saw a beautiful tree in a dream. It wasn't very big but it was full grown. It had a thick trunk and it was full of leaves. As I was looking at the tree, I felt like I was being touched very gently all over my face and each touch gently tingled on my skin. It reminded me of the feeling of snow when it gently falls, and as I looked at the tree in my dream I thought it was snowing. But then I realised that it wasn't snow I was feeling on my face. Falling from the sky around the tree were the most beautiful pale pink feathers, and as I watched some were touching my cheeks as they fell. As soon as I realised they were feathers I woke up with a start to find that I could still feel the sensation of the feathers on my face. That amazed me and I knew that the angels were with me because they had given me the proof that I needed. Even so, every now and then they show me in the most wonderful ways that they are with me. Like the time not so long ago when I started working on this book. It was early November and it was usually a cold frosty month. But that particular week it was very sunny and mild. I let my rabbits out of their hutch to have the run of the garden and I put my guinea pigs in their run. We had had a few foxes in the garden so I took the net curtain down from my window so I had a clear view of my animals. I sat indoors writing and after about an hour I kept getting the urge to go out into the garden. I really wanted to get on with what I was doing so I ignored the urge as I could see there were no foxes around. Time and time the urge came but each time I ignored it. Then suddenly I heard a voice say *"Bring the guinea pigs in for a cuddle."* I said in my mind I'll do it in a minute. Again the voice came and said *"Bring the guinea pigs in for a cuddle."* This time I put my net book down and went outside to the guinea pigs. As I walked up to their pen something made me look up into the sky. The sky was mostly clear apart from the odd cloud, but right up above me was a huge white wispy cloud and it was in the shape of a huge white feather. It didn't just look like a feather, it was one. It even had the quill running through the middle. I knew then why spirit had wanted me to come out into the garden and I felt a little sheepish about taking so long to do so. For me it was more proof that the angels were with me. I rushed back indoors and picked up my mobile phone to take a photo. I sent it to my friends and it's permanently on my phone, and if ever I feel upset I look at my picture and I know all will be well.

I had bought a beautiful piece of crystal at a psychic fair I was working at. It was called honeycomb calcite and it was beautiful. It was oblong in shape and about three inches long and one inch thick. It was a delicate translucent honey gold. As I looked into the crystal I could see rainbows within it and many pictures of my guides as well. As with all crystals, I washed it to cleanse it and placed it on the window sill to energize it. The first time I used it I was lying on the bed and I placed the crystal on my stomach with my hand over the top. I felt myself lifting up slowly and flying through the air. The next thing I knew I was in a room that was dimly lit. I was an angel, but an angel child with wings and a floating gown. There was another child angel with me as well. In the room there was a boy in a hospital bed. He was about 5 years old and he was ill in a coma. There was a doctor in a white coat leaning on a cabinet and he was writing notes with his back towards the boy. The angel and I seemed to be friends and we were giving healing to the boy in the bed. Suddenly the boy started to come out of the coma. We called the doctor but he couldn't hear us so my angel friend ran over to the doctor and started to pull at his sleeve. The doctor couldn't see us of course but he felt something when my angel friend pulled at his clothing. As he turned around he looked down and then he saw that the boy in the bed was starting to sit up. With a huge smile on his face, he walked over to the boy and spoke to him and held his hand. We left the room and flew back to my bedroom and I asked the angel what his name was. *Sandalphon,* he replied. I asked him why we had to appear as children and he said that it was in case the little boy saw us. He wouldn't be frightened if we were children. I opened my eyes and I was lying on my bed with the crystal. In my bedroom there was a large orb which was green and blue. It floated about 4ft of off the floor and then suddenly shot through my window. Later as I said my prayers I thanked God for the wonderful experience I had been allowed to remember.

Chapter 29
Unicorns

If only everyone could see what was really around them, it would bring so much joy to their lives. You only have to open your heart to see the sunshine and the wonderful spiritual beings that are waiting there for us to acknowledge them and ask for their help. They include the most wonderful creatures of our myths and legends. These are the beings that our young children believe in from fairy tales. One type of these beautiful creatures is the unicorns, and once again I have been given the proof of them in the most wonderful ways. I had been visited by a unicorn in a dream one night; it was a very quick dream that only lasted for a few minutes. But it left me with a sense of wonder when I awoke, and for a couple of weeks I couldn't get it out of my mind. All I could think about was that I wanted a unicorn. I felt really stupid, after all I was forty-five years old not 4. But as I said I couldn't get away from that thought. Then one day as I was doing my weekly shop at the local supermarket, I happened to walk past a shelf full of toys. There in front of me was a children's bag in the form of a unicorn. It was beautiful so I bought the bag and took it home and put it on display in my bedroom. That satisfied me, and I thought no more about it until one weekend we took the boys to Mote Park in Maidstone. It was a beautiful sunny day and as Gary and the boys rode around the huge park on their bikes. I sat on a grass slope that overlooked the lake. It was so peaceful, the breeze was gently blowing and I could hear the ducks and birds around me. I lay back on the grass and looked up at the small fluffy clouds floating slowly by. I wasn't thinking about anything at all. My mind was clear of thought which very rarely happened. As I looked at a cloud it started to change shape. The cloud had developed into the shape of a unicorn's head. I would have said that it was a cloud that looked like a unicorn but as I watched the cloud, there were no uneven edges and everything was precise. Even the horn on the head came to a definite point. This was no strange shaped cloud. I knew this was proof for me, from God, that unicorns existed. I felt so enchanted, like a child who has seen their first Christmas tree with all the lights twinkling.

About two years later, I had been asked by my friend Cathy to come and teach the group in Rochester again. I wondered what on Earth I could teach them as they were all quite advanced and it was getting more and more difficult to find something new to teach them. Just as I was going to ring Cathy and ask for a little more time, my guide told me to do unicorns. Well that didn't go down well with me because apart from the 2 experiences I've just told you about, I didn't know anything about them. I decided to look at the books on the internet to see what I could find. I found a wonderful book about unicorns by Diana Cooper, called The Wonder of Unicorns. As soon as I saw this book I knew it was perfect for what I wanted to know. In her book, Diana teaches so many wonderful things and through her book more beautiful experiences were shown to me.

One morning I went into meditation and I saw the same unicorn that visited me fleetingly in a dream. She was waiting by a pool in a beam of light. She told me that her name was Florence and I felt her nuzzle my face. There was such a feeling of love that came from her as I stroked her neck, I could feel the warmth of her under my hand and it felt like I was being caressed in the softest, gentle energy there was. As I came out of my meditation I had tears in my eyes but they weren't tears of sadness, they were tears of unconditional love that I had felt in my meditation. A week later I did another unicorn meditation and this time Florence and I walked through the woods and came to a unicorn that was lying down. It was so still that my first thought was that it had died and I started to feel an awful sadness coming into my stomach. Then the unicorn on the ground started to move around and I saw that her stomach was moving. Right in front of me she gave birth to a beautiful baby unicorn. She stood up and the baby went to her. Then Florence walked me back through the woods and the meditation ended. A few weeks went by and I had an out of body experience. I was asleep and I felt the usual vibration running through my body and I started to lift upwards. I found myself standing in my bathroom and, although I couldn't see anyone with me, I could feel their energy behind me. Suddenly I could hear a noise coming up the stairs towards me. I saw a gnome type creature and a baby unicorn running playfully up the stairs. I was sure that the baby unicorn was the one I had seen before in my meditation. The unicorn looked at me and started growling, this unsettled me and then I heard a voice telling me not to worry. The voice said "He is your protector and he is not growling at you but at the person who is with you." He was warning the person with me not to harm me. As I said before, I've no idea who was with me but I could feel their presence. I woke up in my bed and I was thinking about the baby unicorn. I wondered if he had a name and as soon as I thought that I was given the name Trotsky. I began seeing both of my unicorns more frequently. And with the information that I had found out from Diana's book, I had plenty to teach my friends. Then one morning as I was in the bath daydreaming, I was thinking that I would have to get some more business cards done as I was getting low. I started thinking about my unicorns, I thought I would ask my brother, if between us, we could make a business card design with a unicorn on it, then I thought I would like a rainbow on it as well. My brother has a very busy life, working hard as a lorry driver and I knew that it would take a while for him to find the time. So, when I got out of the bath, I went downstairs and looked on the website where I had ordered cards before. I started looking through the pages and then to my amazement, I saw the business card I wanted. It had a unicorn on it and a rainbow just like I had pictured in the bath. You may say it was coincidence but I really do feel that it was guidance from my spirit friends.

Florence has now become my guide for this stage of my journey and I hear her whenever I feel sad or worried. I have asked her if she will appear in my garden and I know one day she will. Like everything that is wonderful and worthwhile, it comes when you least expect it. It lifts your heart as high as the sky and tears of joy flow down your cheeks as you find that God is in your garden too.